UNLOCKING INFINITY:

MASTER THE ART OF LONGEVITY

Learn How to Boost Your Brain Health, Recharge Your Immune System and Restore Youthful Balance in 3 Easy Steps

Chrio Zoë

<u>Disclaimer Notice:</u>

Please note the information contained within this document is for educational and entertainment purposes only. All effort has been executed to present accurate, up to date, reliable, complete information. No warranties of any kind are declared or implied. Readers acknowledge that the author is not engaged in the rendering of legal, financial, medical or professional advice. The content within this book has been derived from various sources. Please consult a licensed professional before attempting any techniques outlined in this book.

First edition

ACKNOWLEDGEMENT

Writing this book has been a labor and a journey that I couldn't have undertaken without the incredible support and encouragement of many individuals. I am profoundly grateful to all those who have played a part in bringing this project to fruition.

I would like to thank each person who was instrumental in shaping my path to writing this manuscript. My sincerest appreciation goes to the countless friends and family who graciously gave me space and time to make this book become a reality.

First and foremost, I want to express my deepest gratitude to my family whose unwavering belief in me and constant encouragement have been my driving force. Your love and support have sustained me through the challenges of this creative process. I give honor to my late parents, whose unwavering belief has been the catalyst to propel me in this journey. Their constant encouragement and unconditional love have been my strength to pursue this endeavor. I say thank you to my siblings Michael, Anthony, Pauline and Sharon who have now passed on but are the silent voices that ignited me to write this book. Through their life, in their own small contributing way, I have come to realize that this journey we call life is valuable and how we start the journey does not dictate how we finish it.

I would like to thank all of my mentors and teachers who helped me by sharing their invaluable knowledge base with me, as they guided me from a place of knowing in shaping my ideas and refining my writing. I cherish your warm guidance, encouragement, and belief in me, and my potential and I can attest to the fact that it has been transformative. I am sincerely hoping that this book will serve as a helpful resource and companion guide on my readers' journey toward self-improvement, empowerment, and fulfillment.

I'd also like to thank the team at AIA and Publishing Services for their dedication and hard work in bringing this book to life. Your expertise coaching and guidance in outlining, design, formatting, and marketing have been pivotal in turning my manuscript into a polished publication.

Additionally, I am grateful to my dear friends, who provided much-needed moral support and encouragement during the writing process. I am forever grateful for your influence and for your push to encourage me into what you believe I could be. Thank you all for the guidance and the wisdom you shared with me as I stumbled along my sometimes-rocky road of personal growth and self-discovery. I extend my heartfelt appreciation to my friends and colleagues who provided valuable feedback, engaged in insightful discussions, and cheered me on during moments of doubt. Your enthusiasm has been contagious and uplifting.

Finally, I want to acknowledge my readers—those who will engage with this book. Your curiosity and interest in my ideas fuel my passion for writing, and I hope this book resonates with you in meaningful ways. In writing this book, I've come to realize that the journey is made sweeter by the presence of supportive souls. To all those I've mentioned and to anyone whose name might have been inadvertently omitted, please know that your impact has been immeasurable.

To all of you, your enthusiasm, engagement, and support to me have been more than appreciated. Let me end by saying once again to my readers that I applaud you for buying this book to enhance and empower your personal development. I trust that this book will meet your desire.

With heartfelt thanks,

Chrío Zoë

Contents

ACKNOWLEDGEMENT v

INTRODUCTION 1

The Infinity Sign Is a Symbol of Boundlessness That Transcends Time
....5

Part 1: THE LONGEVITY SOCIETY 9

Chapter 1: Why Live a Long Life—The Human Desire of a Life That's Well-Lived..11

The Pursuit of Infinity 14

Key Takeaway Points..22

Chapter 2: What Makes You Old—The Science of Aging and Growth.....25

The Four Dimensions of Aging 27

Key Takeaway Points..42

Chapter 3: How Technology Is Reshaping the Future of Longevity..........45

The Longevity Society and the Revolution of Technology 45

Smart Bandages 49

Key Takeaway Points..50

Part 2: MASTERING YOUR 3 INFINITY ZONES IS AS EASY AS A.B.C.
....51

Chapter 4: Infinity Zone 1—Anima 53

The Infinite Potential of Your Anima 55

The Power of Positive Thinking 58

The Health Benefits of Positive Thinking 59

Ways to Identify Negative Thinking...60

How to Focus on Positive Thinking 61

Engage in Gratitude and Mindfulness Exercises.............................63

A List of Gratitude Exercises 64

List of Mindfulness Exercises..66

Unlocking the Anima Infinity Zone 68

Additional Ways to Nourish Your Soul 70

Debunking Myths 75

Key Takeaway Points 81

Making Knowledge Infinite 83

Chapter 5: Infinity Zone 2—Body 85

Unlocking the Body Infinity Zone 87

Science-Based Techniques to Increase Gut Bacteria 90

An In-Depth Look at How Alcohol Can Affect Your Body 94

Short-term Effects of Alcohol 95

Long-term Effects of Alcohol 96

Alcohol's Physical Effects on Your Body 97

Alcohol Use During Pregnancy Is a Big NO! 101

Psychological Effects of Excessive Drinking 102

Alcohol Safety Tips You Can Follow 105

Debunking Myths 106

Key Takeaway Points 107

Chapter 6: Infinity Zone 3—Community 109

Unlocking the Community Infinity Zone 112

Things to Keep in Mind 114

Debunking Myths 115

Key Takeaway Points 117

Chapter 7: Putting Together the A.B.C. of Infinity 119

Creating Your Longevity Plan 120

Key Takeaway Points 123

Part 3: LEARNING FROM THOSE WHO LIVED THE LIFE.................**125**

Chapter 8: Lessons From the Blue Zones—The Secrets of Long-Lived Communities.. 127

Five Blue Zones That Have the Healthiest People.............................. 128

The Blue Zone Way of Life.. 129

Key Takeaway Points... 133

Chapter "Good Will"..**135**

Chapter 9: Tales of Youth, Vibrance, and Contentment........................... 137

The Living Legends of Longevity.. 137

Quick Tips From Centenarians... 139

Additional Statistics You Will Find Interesting 140

Years of Wisdom... 141

CONCLUSION **145**

The Most Important Things to Remember Regarding Longevity 146

Longevity Increases by Practicing Meditation.................................... 152

Foods to Eat That Can Contribute to Your Longevity 153

Don't Forget to Embrace Positive Thinking 156

Chapter "Good Will"..**159**

SPREAD THE WORD!...**161**

REFERENCES...**163**

ABOUT THE AUTHOR **177**

INTRODUCTION

Living a longer and more satisfying life has become a generally shared desire at a time when people are living longer than ever before. A new way of living, the Longevity Society, has emerged as a result of medical advancements, changing lifestyle trends, and a shared desire for youth and vigor. You have a lot of obligations because the world is moving at such a rapid pace today. You desire to have the opportunity to enjoy life and make priceless memories in the middle of all of that. Nobody wants to work for the rest of their lives and look back on it, regretting that they did not truly enjoy their lives or that they reached a certain age and missed the chance to do certain things. Many of you who are reading this are anxious about different things, which is natural. The fear of death is genuine, as is the worry that you will not have lived your life to the fullest. The possibility of dying from accidents or illnesses is another unforeseen possibility that confounds many of you. It is not unusual or pessimistic to think this way; everyone has these moments of reflection from time to time, whether they wish to admit it or not. Everyone understands that death will never be predicted; no one can anticipate when it will happen. However, many of you who are reading this have the desire to exert every effort to have as much control over your lives as you can and live them to the fullest. While struggling with the dread of dying is one aspect, the aging process is another issue that affects us all. I think it is reasonable to suggest that you would be insulted if someone told you that you appeared older than you are. Not only would it be upsetting, but that one phrase may also invoke feelings of insecurity, especially if you have a friend or relative who is your age but appears younger than their actual age. You may find that you start to compare yourself to them (which you should never do). I don't want any of you to let other people's opinions have that kind of impact on you.

Additionally, as you get older, you can experience new challenges, such as joint discomfort and other disorders that commonly appear as you get older. I want every one of you to know that I am aware of how you are feeling, which is why I chose to write this book. There is a solution to deal with these issues, and I'll outline the adjustments you can make to not only lengthen your life but also slow down the aging process since there are several aspects that affect longevity and aging that you can control. I am aware of your shared desire for a fresh start.

You want to get rid of everything that is getting in your way, including undesirable or unhealthy lifestyle choices.

I believe that each of you wants to drastically alter your life in some way in order to ensure a bright, healthy future. In my book, I will explore the 3 Infinity Zone Method of Longevity, which simplifies the process of learning how to live a long life into three simple stages:

- focusing on the mind and soul (anima)

- focusing on the body

- focusing on social health and building a health-conscious environment and community.

The ideas presented in this book are supposed to "transcend time," so you may continue to benefit from them as you get older and wiser.

The Infinity Sign Is a Symbol of Boundlessness That Transcends Time

The meaning of the infinity sign is deeply rooted in spirituality, love, beauty, and majesty. The sign evokes awe and amazement due to the enchantment of our history and the potential for an everlasting future. It stands for simplicity and balance in a world full of distractions and difficulties. It serves as a reminder to be aware of our surroundings and the countless opportunities that lie ahead of us. What does the infinity sign imply, though? Where does infinity come from? (Infinity Symbol Meaning in Modern Times, 2019) A mathematical representation of the idea of endless possibilities is the infinity sign, often known as the lemniscate (lem-nis-cate). It resembles a sideways figure eight and has influenced contemporary culture, art, and spirituality in addition to mathematical calculations, which are all part of our daily lives. The symbol has evolved over time to represent a variety of ideas that go beyond arithmetic and philosophy.

The unlimited sign has several symbolic meanings depending on the situation, such as:

- **Endlessness or eternity**: The sign, as its name implies, stands for everything that has no beginning or end.

- **Empowerment**: The lemniscate serves as a reminder that, despite any obstacles, we are still capable of doing great things and that our capacity for achievement is unbounded.

- **Balance**: The design is a special fusion of two independent yet linked loops. It represents balance, duality, and connections between seemingly conflicting energies or things, such as life and mortality, light versus dark, or affection and enmity.

- **Oneness**: Because it is endless and unbreakable, the infinity symbol effectively conveys the idea of the eternal connection that exists between all things in the cosmos (Steven, 2013).

- **Love that never ends**: Since eternity lasts forever, love that never ends may touch us just once and last a lifetime, holding onto us till we pass away. While it is impossible to fully comprehend the idea of infinity or being genuinely eternal, it symbolizes the desire for anything, like love or a connection, to remain forever. The notion of being "together forever" is embodied by the two interlocking rings, each of which represents a side of the partnership.

- **Harmony**: If there is conflict inside you or with others, it may also be quite helpful in resolving it. In this manner, it teaches us how to comprehend how opposites that appear to be incompatible can be brought together. It aids us in gaining a fresh viewpoint on issues that seem intractable.

- **Healing powers**: It can aid in healing. The lemniscate can be used as a symbol on any portion of the body where harmony and balance are required by picturing or sketching it.

- **Assists with decision-making**: A complete loop with no beginning or end, the infinity sign can provide you with limitless energy if you find yourself in a difficult circumstance. This symbol is helpful for making decisions. It is also regarded as a potent technique in kinesiology and is applied to unite the left and right hemispheres of the brain, giving balance to a person's entire being, including their mind, body, and soul.

- **Renewal**: life arises from death, and with destruction, endless cycles of regeneration are created. This is known as the circle of life.

- **Ultimate power**: Infinity serves as a constant reminder that there are no bounds. There are countless choices, yet neither our actions nor our location are constrained.

- **A figure bigger than the greatest number that is possible**: Its form is reminiscent of the number 8. In a religious setting, the number 8 represents the initiates, or individuals who have successfully completed all seven waking phases and all seven heavenly realms. Additionally, the power of resurrection and regeneration energy, which represent bliss and paradise, is connected to infinity's spiritual meaning. It is a symbol of riches and success in Chinese culture and is employed in Feng Shui to create harmonious living environments (Roiss, 2020).

The boundless sign has taken on a variety of shapes and interpretations outside of these fundamental connotations in diverse contexts (Steven, 2013). My book includes a communal aspect that, although an essential component of longevity, is rarely covered in other books. The key to releasing "infinity" will be revealed to you. You will gain knowledge on how to regulate the variables under your control and comprehend how to lead long, healthy lives that are full of purpose. My goal is not to overwhelm you but to enlighten you and provide you with the knowledge that will enable you to achieve longevity and tranquility. I will go deeply into the Three Infinity Zone Method, which I will make simple to follow and understand because it draws on the idea of infinity and focuses on releasing your endless potential to achieve a healthy body and mind.

Part 1

THE LONGEVITY SOCIETY

Chapter 1

Why Live a Long Life—The Human Desire of a Life That's Well-Lived

The idea of defeating death has attracted humans for ages. A powerful allure of religion, art, and popular ideas has been immortality, perpetual youth, or at the very least, the possibility of attaining biblical age. The one fundamental concept of almost all faiths since Ancient Egypt is life after death, which is essentially endless life. Some of the patriarchs, in the Old Testament, are to be believed to have lived for many hundreds of years. The notion of the fountain of youth was quite prevalent in medieval times, and it was frequently depicted in artwork, such as Lucas Cranach's The Fountain of Youth. And society today still finds immortality fascinating, as seen by the numerous Hollywood films and books that explore the topic (Hall, 2005). Age is a cultural construct, much like youth or sexuality. Ancient life expectancy was different from modern life expectancy. Many ancient Greeks lived to be elderly but were still active and productive. The list is extremely impressive, and many of the individuals on it were outstanding in later life. For instance, the reputed 157-year lifespan of Epimenides of Crete, a renowned prophet and seer.

The most notable candidate was Epimenides if age is the primary requirement. The eminent rhetorician Gorgias lived to be 108 and is another well-known Greek who outlived a century. The famous tragic poet Sophocles is another name worth mentioning. He composed his final play, Oedipus at Colonus, at the age of 90, and it happens to be a piece that deals extensively with aging. It is noteworthy that these people lived lengthy lives, providing insight into old age in ancient Greece, when there was nothing shameful about getting older. Being elderly, according to the Ancient Greeks, was nothing to be embarrassed about.

They saw longevity as a sign of knowledge and outstanding intelligence, and they took great pleasure in their age. The fundamental reason for this was that in ancient Greece, there were not many elderly individuals. Being old was like being a member of an elite club to them. Walking around the streets of ancient cities like Greece, Rome, Egypt, or any other country during that time period, you would find relatively few elderly individuals compared to now. To put it another way, there would have been significantly fewer elderly people since individuals aged far faster in ancient times, as is true today in places where people live harsher lives than in the West. More than 15% of the population in the United States and the United Kingdom is over the age of 65, and this proportion is expected to climb. It is now at 25% in Japan, and it is anticipated to reach 30% by 2030. In certain countries, women have a life expectancy of roughly 80 years, while men have a life expectancy of 75 years. Compared to today, the percentage of individuals who lived into their fifties, much less their sixties, seventies, or eighties, was substantially lower in ancient and medieval times.

Humans will always be captivated by the urge to live longer and will always look for strategies and techniques to do so. This is not a novel hypothesis, and in ancient Rome and Greece, people attempted a variety of methods to lengthen their lives. According to the ancient historian Moses Finley, he thought that the type of wine one drank had a significant impact on how long a person lived. He said that the Romans preserved their wine with sapa, a substance that resembled syrup. They cooked it over a fire in metallic pots by heating freshly squeezed grape juice that retained the seeds and stem of the grapes. But they were methodically poisoning themselves. In addition, this procedure would have reduced their fertility. The Greeks, on the other hand, preserved food using a safe resin ingredient. Retsina, a drink that is still consumed today, contains it. Finley came to the conclusion that the Greeks lived longer than the Romans as a result of this. Although it is a fascinating notion based on alcohol, there isn't any concrete data to support it. The environment, food, profession, physical well-being, and mental acuity are among the elements that lead to a long life, according to a book wrongly attributed to the satirist Lucian called The Long-Lived Ones. This demonstrates that there are additional elements that impact longevity besides just eating and drinking well (Garland, 2020).

The Pursuit of Infinity

There are more people living longer than ever before, but this wasn't always the case. Major advancements in medicine throughout the years have led to numerous changes in our way of life. The present public health system has been molded by two forces during the past 150 years: First, the expansion of scientific knowledge about the causes and methods of illness management; and second, the expansion of public acceptance of disease control as a possibility and a shared obligation. In past ages, when little was understood about the causes of sickness, society tended to view illness with a certain amount of resignation, and few public measures were taken. More efficient countermeasures against health dangers were created as our understanding of the causes of disease, and ways to control them improved. For the purpose of using recently developed interventions against health hazards, public organizations, and agencies were established. Public authorities increased as a result of the advancement of scientific knowledge and took on additional responsibilities such as regulation, sanitation, immunization, health education, and personal health care. Science, the creation of interventions, and the structure of public authorities to use interventions all contributed to greater public awareness of and societal commitment to promoting health. The development of a public health protection system required both scientific advancement and societal change. Public efforts to reduce suffering and pain become possible thanks to the medical understanding and societal perceptions of the importance of this objective. In order to create a strategy for addressing health issues, knowledge, and values have been brought together in the public sphere throughout the history of the public health system. Epidemics like the plague, cholera, and smallpox throughout recorded history have prompted periodic public initiatives to save civilians from terrifying illnesses.

A public effort was undertaken to stop the spread of a specific epidemic sickness by quarantining travelers and isolating the sick, despite the fact that epidemic disease was frequently seen as a symptom of a low moral and religious condition that needed to be remedied through prayer and devotion. In the latter half of the seventeenth century, public officials were established in a number of European cities to implement and enforce quarantine and isolation rules. By the seventeenth century, quarantining those who had been exposed and isolating those who were ill had become standard practices for limiting specific dangerous illnesses. Many American port communities have enacted regulations for commerce quarantine and sick-person isolation. Massachusetts implemented regulations in 1701 requiring the isolation of smallpox patients and the occasional ship quarantine. Cities started establishing public institutions for the treatment of the mentally ill and volunteer general hospitals for the physically ill in the seventeenth century. Last but not least, neighbors in nearby areas took care of their dependents who were physically and psychologically ill. With the passage of the Poor Law in England in 1601, this practice became law, and it persisted throughout the American colonies.

Public health made significant progress during the nineteenth century. The major hygienic revolution (Winslow, 1923): A key element of nineteenth-century social changes was the recognition of filth as a source of disease and a means of transmission, followed by the embrace of cleanliness. Sanitation altered how people in society viewed health. It evolved into a belief that illness was a sign of unhealthy social, environmental, moral, and spiritual circumstances. It was accepted that maintaining cleanliness would lead to both psychological and physical well-being. In order to assist the populace in avoiding sickness, cleanliness, piety, and seclusion were considered complementary and mutually reinforcing strategies. Mental health facilities changed their focus to "moral treatment" and recovery at the same time. Additionally, sanitization altered how society viewed government oversight of citizens' health. Health preservation became a societal obligation. Epidemics remained the main emphasis of disease management, but the approach changed from isolating and quarantining the individual to sanitizing and enhancing the communal environment. And the focus of disease control switched from responding to sporadic outbreaks to maintaining preventive measures. Sanitation has made public health a societal objective and health protection a public responsibility (The Future of Public Health, 1988). I mention all of this to help you completely understand that nobody chose to pass away young or spend their 20s in bed recovering from an illness. That was just one of many things that altered the way we went about doing various things, which ultimately played a crucial role in helping many people live longer and more productive lives. Humans will always be interested in how long they can live and how long they can enjoy healthy and happy lives.

Social policy spent most of the 20th century trying to extend people's lives, but in more recent years, the emphasis has shifted to exploring ways to prolong a good life or health span. The tremendous rise in life expectancy during the last century may be the greatest human achievement. As life expectancy nearly doubled, the world underwent a significant transition in one century, going from having practically no countries with a life expectancy of more than 50 years to several countries with a life expectancy of 80 years. For instance, in the United States, the life expectancy at birth increased from 47.3 to 78.7 during the course of 110 years, from 1900 to 2010. This longer lifespan was first brought on by decreases in infectious diseases and mortality that affected disproportionately young people. Cardiovascular diseases and cancer became the leading causes of mortality after infectious diseases accounted for the majority of deaths. In the second half of the 20th century, those diseases became the focus of science and medicine. In the last decades of the 20th century, life expectancy continued to rise, mostly as a result of reduced heart disease mortality. Recent gains in life expectancy have occurred at older ages since heart disease is the leading cause of death in older people. The range of life expectancy has grown all the way up to 100 years, for sure. The probability that we will live to be 100 years old has increased with time, both in the United States and in other countries. The number of centenarians has increased every ten years since 1960 in Japan, the nation with the highest life expectancy at the moment. Even though estimates from the Social Security Administration of the United States from the period life table for 2010 show significant percentage increases, only about 1% of people are estimated to live to 100 years old; this number is projected to rise to about 8% for the cohort of 2100, which is still a very low percentage. Because death rates are exceptionally high at very old ages and often rise exponentially as individuals age, relatively few people reach the century mark. In Japan, the rate of centenarian deaths has decreased, but only slightly—from around 50% annually to 35% annually. There is now relatively little improvement in overall life expectancy at birth due to increases in mortality over age 100 since so few people live to reach that age and because they have a very low life expectancy at that age. Whether there is a physiological maximum limit to life expectancy that we cannot transcend determines whether the percentage of individuals living to 100 and life expectancy will climb significantly at the oldest ages (Crimmins, 2015).

From an Aging Society to a Longevity Society

Global aging is an accomplishment of progress made possible by quick rises in life expectancy. Governments, people, homes, communities, and businesses face both new possibilities and difficulties as a result of it. To handle these issues and profit from the societal and financial advantages of aging, countries must modify their social protection and employment laws and programs. Future wealth and harmony in society will depend on their capacity to adapt. The threats to economic development and fiscal stability caused by the declining working-age population, the necessity to provide amenities and advantages to an aging population, and the hazards of increasing disparities and social unrest are the main concerns that are often used to define the aging issue.

Even while these concerns exist, society's aging can also offer benefits and the chance to lessen risks. Additionally, this is not solely a goal for more established developing countries. Younger countries must also prepare themselves for the population shift. Global aging can become a source of equitable economic growth with the help of timely policy measures. Additionally, it can benefit everyone by facilitating labor mobility across countries that are at various phases of demographic change, for instance. Prior to being seen as economic players, older people must first be regarded as humans. Additionally, they are not a uniform bunch. By concentrating on social isolation, elder abuse, and age-based discrimination, policies need to accommodate their unique and changing needs and defend their rights. The financial and societal contributions of older people as employees, caretakers, volunteers, and donors of money must also be acknowledged and valued. They are also important sources of social legitimacy and norms. In addition, societal aging may provide new market possibilities, jobs, and innovation with the correct balance of policies and institutional backing (Societal Aging, 2022). In light of this, attention must shift away from an aging society and toward a longevity society as the population demographic transition enters a new stage of longevity. A longevity society aims to take advantage of the benefits of living longer through changes in how we age, as opposed to an aging society, which concentrates on changes in the population's age structure. The life cycle and social norms must undergo significant change in order to create a society that lives longer. This transformation in epidemiology toward a focus on postponing age-related problems is also necessary. A significant healthcare agenda aimed at avoiding increases in health disparities, the creation of longevity committees to guarantee synchronized policy across government agencies, and intergenerational assessment of policies are just a few of the broad changes necessary to achieve healthy longevity. These changes also include a greater emphasis on healthy life expectancy and a shift from intervention to preventive health. If society wants to make the most of the extra time that longevity affords, it must rethink deeply held beliefs about age and aging. A longevity society symbolizes a new stage for mankind (Scott, 2021).

A person is considered to have longevity if they live longer than the typical individual. Longevity is the pursuit of your highest possible age. By putting healthy habits and attitudes into practice, this may be possible to achieve. I think it's extremely likely that humans will live considerably longer than we now think. If people can establish the optimum circumstances of a good diet and exercise, they may live longer. So, you might be wondering what influences my longevity. You might believe that your genes control how long you live, but in reality, genetics only contribute up to 30% of life expectancy. The remainder is determined by your actions, attitudes, and surroundings.

What should you do to enhance your longevity and surpass the average? Here is a list of things to consider:

❖ **Get frequent exercise**: According to research, moderate exercise done often can literally turn back the hands of time on your DNA.

❖ **Put a lot of vegetables on your plate**: Almost every diet believes that eating more vegetables is the best course of action, despite the various disagreements around the optimum diet for extending a lifetime.

❖ **Think about intermittent fasting**: This can be done in many different ways. Mice's lifespans (and health) have been found to be greatly extended by fasting. Caloric restriction increases the lifespan of mice and other test species, according to research that dates back to the 1930s. In a 2018 study that was published in Cell Metabolism, 53 non-obese adult humans were followed for two years. 15% fewer calories were consumed by the test group. According to metabolic investigations, the test group exhibited less oxidative stress/damage than the control group.

❖ **Get adequate rest**: When they receive between seven and nine hours of sleep every night, most people feel their best.

❖ **Take care to control your tension**: Stress may have negative impacts on your body and encourage negative habits like smoking or binge eating.

❖ **Develop your interpersonal interactions**: Being around our loved ones seems to increase longevity, maybe because it reduces stress or hazardous conduct. According to a study conducted by academics at the University of Exeter Medical School in England, volunteers had a 22% lower death rate than non-volunteers.

❖ **Avoid overusing alcohol and smoking**: Avoid using tobacco products and abusing alcohol.

Today, resolve to make one healthy adjustment each week. You'll soon feel better and be headed toward a long life (Stibich, 2023).

Key Takeaway Points

> ➢ The infinity symbol has several symbolic meanings: endlessness or eternity, empowerment, balance, oneness, love that never ends, harmony, healing powers, decision-making, renewal, ultimate power, and a figure bigger than the greatest number possible.

> ➢ The meaning of the infinity symbol encompasses spirituality, love, beauty, and power. The number infinity stands for simplicity and balance in a world full of distractions and difficulties. It serves as a reminder of our current location and the seemingly endless opportunities that lie ahead of us. The symbol stands for the limitless and incalculable.

> ➢ Many people think that a person's life expectancy is mostly determined by their genetic makeup. However, the role of genes is far less substantial than previously believed. Environmental factors, such as diet and lifestyle, emerge as crucial.

I will go into more detail on the science of aging and growth in the following chapter and give you more context. According to evolutionary theories, somatic maintenance constraints that have evolved over time that enable harm to accumulate rather than active gene programming are what lead to aging. The compromises between investing in growth, reproduction, and somatic survival are influenced by ecological factors, including hazard rates and food availability, which helps to explain why different species have evolved to have various life spans and why the aging rate may occasionally be changed, for example by dietary restriction. Understanding the many mechanisms that cause damage to build up and the intricate web of systems that seek to prevent harm means understanding the cell and molecular foundations of aging (Kirkwood, 2005).

Chapter 2

What Makes You Old—The Science of Aging and Growth

In terms of biological processes, aging is likely the most well-known yet least understood. Each of us learns rapidly about the impacts of aging, first by witnessing what it causes others and later by personally experiencing them. The majority of people have a notion about why and how aging occurs. But most of these notions are mostly, if not completely, wrong. The first peculiarity is a common but incorrect tendency, which is to think of aging as being predetermined. As I will demonstrate, there is little evidence to support the establishment of such an initiative, and there are strong justifications for why it shouldn't. Therefore, much of the peculiarity of aging research comes from the necessity of starting by challenging crucial beliefs about why aging happens. The second peculiarity of aging is its inherently complicated nature. With age, almost every feature of an organism's phenotype changes, and this phenomenological diversity has, throughout time, given rise to a confusing number of theories concerning particular cellular and molecular causes. Fortunately, recent developments have resulted in a simplification of the theoretical foundations of aging research that has made it easier to investigate the phenomenological complexity of the senescent phenotype. The inherent complexity of aging, however, continues to be a major obstacle to knowing what causes it. The theory is unusually crucial to studies on aging since it arises from non-intuitive causes and develops in complicated ways. I will investigate and critically evaluate the present scientific and philosophical underpinnings of why and how aging occurs. The field of developmental biology, which is increasingly viewed as crucial for understanding health and illness, must be explored in order to answer the question of why aging happens. The difficulty for evolutionary theory in the case of aging is to explain why aging happens despite its clear disadvantages. A typical definition of aging is a gradual, widespread degradation of function that makes a person more vulnerable to external stressors and increases their risk of illness and mortality. A reduction in fertility is frequently seen along with it. As a result, aging is linked to significant age-related losses in Darwinian fitness, raising the question of why natural selection has not combated this phenomenon more forcefully (Kirkwood, 2005).

The Four Dimensions of Aging

Biological Aging Versus Chronological Aging

The four dimensions of aging are chronological, biological, psychological, and social. Given that many people frequently conflate the two, I must discuss chronological and biological aging together. In reality, your biological age differs from your chronological age. As opposed to biological age, which is determined by physiological evidence, chronological age is the duration of your existence. Your biological age might be younger than your chronological age if you're very physically fit and healthy for your age. However, your biological age may be higher if you are inactive, have a chronic illness, or are in poor physical condition. According to studies, biological age predicts the start of disease and mortality more accurately than chronological age. Your actual age cannot be changed. You were born on a specific day and have been alive for a specific period of time. Even if you desire to, you cannot alter that. But you've probably met a few folks whose chronological age startled you because they seemed or "seemed" considerably older or younger than their actual age. Their chronological age may not accurately reflect their biological age. Biological age, sometimes referred to as physiological age or functional age, is a reflection of your level of health. Cells and tissues throughout the body experience buildup as a result. Knowing your biological age might help you forecast your risk of developing old-age illnesses and your mortality. Organs in your body age differently. The biological age of each of your organs varies. For instance, a person who spends a lot of time staring at screens but also maintains a healthy diet and engages in regular exercise might possess eyes with an elevated biological age and a heart with a lower biological age. Age is measured chronologically, whereas age is measured biologically, and the latter may be reversed (Basaraba, 2023).

Why Is Your Biological Age Important?

Knowing your biological age is the first step to knowing your health profile. The biological age tells you how much of your body's cellular and metabolic processes have been harmed. It is more accurate than chronological age at predicting age-related illnesses like diabetes, cardiovascular diseases, and mortality risk. Your body may be aging appropriately if your biological age and your actual age are equal. But let's say your biological age is younger than your age in years. If so, it means that your body is aging less quickly than the body of an average person your age would. On the other hand, if your biological age is older than your chronological age, your body is not functioning as well as it should. You might be interested in learning more about your biological makeup after reading this. According to research, there are two factors that affect biological age. They include the following:

- ❖ **Telomeres**: A good indication of biological aging is the length of the telomere. Your chromosomes, which contain your genetic material, are shielded by telomeres. A cap is formed at the end of each chromosome by them. Part of this shield is lost each time the cell divides. One of the signs of aging is the shortening of the telomeres, which is the loss of these components. A study found that neurological problems, chronic illnesses, and early mortality are more prevalent in those with shorter telomeres. It's possible that you are physiologically older than someone your own age because you have shorter telomeres. You may stop the shortening of your telomeres by making a number of modifications and taking actions that have been supported by science. For instance, increasing your regular physical activity can aid in telomere lengthening. But since it will vary greatly from person to person, you should first get a telomere length study.

❖ **Deoxyribonucleic acid (DNA) Methylation**: The numerous systems that switch genes on and off in response to your body's requirements cause your DNA to change continuously. DNA methylation is the mechanism used to sustain gene activity. Researchers found that not all tissues were the same age after analyzing the DNA methylation of more than 8,000 samples of various human organs and tissues. This demonstrates how different body parts mature at various rates. Your cumulative biological age is predicted by the average biological age of every single organ in your entire body (Abedi, 2023).

Your Biological Age is Affected by a Number of Factors

Contrary to popular belief, you do have some influence over some aspects of your biological age. The elements that directly determine your biological age have been better identified. There isn't just one component, and while adopting a healthy lifestyle is wonderful for your body overall, it doesn't always mean that it will make you seem younger biologically. You need to be aware of a few things, though, in order to reverse your biological age.

These elements consist of the following:

- **Genetics**: Your biological age is influenced by genetics, just like every other component of your health. Age-related disorders are directly influenced by some genes. The way these genes are expressed can either increase or decrease your biological age. Over 300 genes associated with human aging are currently included in the GenAge database, and over 500 results from human genetic association studies are available in the LongevityMap database. Premature aging disorders can be brought on by mutations in these genes. While understanding your genetic predispositions might impact your lifestyle choices to increase your lifespan, Deoxyribonucleic acid (DNA) cannot be changed.

- **Diet**: Diet has a major impact on biological aging. Dietary factors can either be pro- or anti-inflammatory. Increasing the consumption of plant-based proteins lowers the risk of cardiovascular disease (CVD) and several of its related indicators, such as glucose, triglycerides, and cholesterol, all of which alter biological aging. A balanced diet with lots of fruits and vegetables and less salt has been linked to a slower aging process and lower a biological age.

- **Exercise**: The body's defense system is strengthened, a healthy body weight is maintained, and the risk of inflammation is decreased through exercise and physical activity. According to studies, those who exercise 150 minutes each week are nine years younger than those who adopt a sedentary lifestyle. According to research, those who include aerobic exercise in their routine are typically 5.5 years younger than inactive individuals.

- **Other elements**: In addition to these, the physical environment, stress, and sleep all have an impact on biological aging. Sleep deprivation has a deleterious effect on biological age and lifespan. Numerous poisons in the environment have the ability to accelerate biological aging (Abedi, 2023).

Psychological Aging

Psychological age is the term used to describe an individual's perceived age or how old they feel. The person's psychological age is determined by how they think, feel, and act; it is not always the same as their actual age. This is apparent in a lot of people; you can come across someone who is chronologically older but acts and thinks much younger than their actual age. They participate in specific actions and habits that might be detrimental to their physical health, such as doing back flips that can damage their joints or even regularly drinking excessive amounts of alcohol during gatherings. Another group of individuals are those whose psychological age is greater than their actual age; you find these people to be very mature and frequently perceive themselves to be older than they actually are. You may discover that they actually exhibit actions that are characteristic of young adults. There is some evidence that these teenagers' social maturity and drive for accomplishment and the frequently authoritative, emotionally loving, democratic, and strict parental environment in which they were nurtured may be related to their advanced psychological age. On the negative side, teens who feel older than they are may get involved in risk-taking that can be problematic and/or harmful (Symons, 2011). In our adult years, psychological aging processes involve alterations to our personalities, cognitive abilities, and sense of self. While certain changes are thought to be a natural component of adult growth, others are the consequence of physiological changes in the way the brain works, and some psychological traits show very little change over time. Similar to physical aging, a great deal of study has examined the intricacies of these processes and methods to separate unique illness processes, such as Alzheimer's disease or depression, from regular aging changes.

A few generalizations are crucial for our objectives. First of all, people do continue to change and advance throughout their lives. Some gerontology researchers are particularly intrigued by the distinctive features of human development in later life—the tasks, development, and adjustments that normally occur throughout time. This text spends a lot of time on the possibilities for later-life growth and contributions to the world. The majority of personality characteristics, as well as self-concept and self-esteem, remain mostly steady from midlife on, according to a second general statement about psychological elements of aging. The cranky old lady, for instance, was probably a cranky young woman; individuals do not become smart, cranky, or inflexible in their views as they age. Although developmental possibilities and difficulties change throughout the course of a person's life, tactics for adjusting to change, strengthening one's sense of self, and working toward the realization of one's full potential are used consistently throughout adulthood. These underlying personality structures and tactics seldom call for or result in substantial changes due to the sheer passage of time. Similarly, declining cognitive abilities are not a necessary part of getting older. Memory and other cognitive abilities may hold steady or even increase with age, just as severe physical function loss is neither inevitable nor universal. However, it is crucial to be precise about age-related changes in this context. According to a recent study on the prevalence of dementia, 37.4% of adults 90 years of age and older had dementia, compared to 5% of people aged 71 to 79. According to this pattern, it is accurate to suggest that aging is a risk factor for dementia but inaccurate to claim that aging causes cognitive decline (Morgan, 2015).

There are some advantages to psychological aging:

❖ It can provide people with perspective on their own growth, maturity, and life experiences, enabling them to identify their own strengths and shortcomings and make wise living choices.

❖ It may also provide people with a sense of control over their lives and aid in the development of worthwhile objectives and plans for the future.

❖ It is possible to determine areas where one may need to grow in order to experience better pleasure and fulfillment by taking into consideration one's psychological age.

❖ Additionally, it can aid individuals in understanding their interactions with others, which can promote improved communication and stronger interpersonal bonds.

Despite its benefits, psychological age has limitations, including the following:

❖ Since it is a biased self-perception, it may be altered by individual emotions and sentiments. Objective and precise measurement is challenging.

❖ Psychological ages can range widely from person to person, making it impossible to compare them across individuals.

❖ As a result of life events, aging, and other circumstances, psychological age can alter over time.

❖ The state of one's mind, emotions, and body may all have an impact on their psychological age.

❖ Environmental elements, such as those in our immediate environment, might also have an impact on it (Psychological Age, 2023).

Social Aging

Why does aging matter in people's lives if aging simply causes relatively minor universal and unavoidable changes in physical or cognitive functioning, in the fundamental make-up of personality, and in the course of adult development? To be frank, the social meanings, institutions, and procedures associated with age are what make it meaningful. Gray hair, wrinkles, slower response times, and even some short-term memory losses are only significant because of how our social environment has classified them as significant traits. False assumptions about how aging affects physical and mental skills account for a large portion of the social meaning of aging. We do not necessarily become inflexible in our thinking as we age, forgetful, or incapable of engaging in our favorite intellectual or physical pursuits. Most of the time, aging is a slow process of change that we can accommodate, and that has minimal effect on our daily lives.

However, age is used by society to assign responsibilities, move people into and out of places within the social structure, determine how resources should be distributed, and categorize people. Using age to distribute opportunities is a sensible approach in its most charitable version. For instance, our society has regulations governing the minimum age for employment. These laws were created to safeguard children from exploitation, and others argue that they are beneficial for the labor force since they regulate the influx of new employees into the labor market. However, aging arbitrarily and unfairly restricts people's options in a more constricting way. Both physical functionality and cognitive capacity are unaffected by gray hair, wrinkles, or the calendar age of 65, which is the most often used definition of old age. However, they have a significant impact on social interactions and possibilities for people in the social spheres of work, family, and community involvement. In reality, our evaluation of a person's age and what that person's age means to us influences whether we would seriously think about them as potential applicants for a job or as an intriguing social companion. It's not that being over 65 or having gray hair indicates competency or ineptitude, that one has a dull or fascinating personality, or even that one is naturally attractive or unattractive.

We make these judgments because the meaning of aging has been shaped by our culture in certain (often unfavorable) ways. It is crucial to consider how well the same processes function at various ages and stages of life. In our society, it is conceivable to be "too young" or "too old" for particular jobs and possibilities. When a person is old enough to drive a vehicle, get married, and serve as president of a country, we have very explicit social prescriptions, frequently in the form of federal and state laws. In many instances, "old enough" appears to refer to the window of opportunity that exists between being socially and legally too old. Therefore, social aging refers to the ways in which society influences how aging is understood and experienced. People's expectations and presumptions about how we should act, what we are like, what we can accomplish, and what we should be doing at certain ages are all part of social aging. In addition, the idea of social aging relates to how such expectations affect the possibilities that become available to us as we age. In the book's latter chapters, the ideas of social aging are applied to the main facets of our social lives, such as families, employment, and health (Morgan, 2015).

Intrinsic Aging Versus Extrinsic Aging

The best methods for promoting healthy aging and maintaining quality of life are still being discovered by science. In particular, the aging of the skin has attracted attention since it is both the most evident sign of aging and a reflection of general human health. The most frequent reason for itchy skin, for example, is dryness. However, itching can also be a sign of an underlying illness; for example, it may be the first sign of cirrhosis or hepatitis. It is common knowledge that aging of the skin is an inevitable occurrence, and there are several factors that might impact it at different times in life. Extrinsic variables like environment and lifestyle are among them, as are intrinsic elements like biology and physique (Caturla, 2021).

The skin ages due to both intrinsic and extrinsic aging processes, as it is the largest organ of the body and is constantly in contact with the outside world. Wrinkling, elasticity loss, laxity, and the appearance of rough texture are characteristics of aging skin. Skin cells' phenotypes change along with this aging process, and extracellular matrix elements like collagen and elastin also undergo structural and functional modifications. I will be highlighting these skin aging changes, the molecular processes behind these modifications, and the therapeutic approaches used to delay or reverse skin aging. The skin serves as a physical barrier between the body and the outside world. In addition to guarding against water loss and microbial infection, it serves an essential aesthetic function. People's social behavior and reproductive status may benefit from looking young and attractive. But organ aging starts the moment a person is born, and the skin is not an exception. As the largest organ in the body, the skin ages most visibly and obviously as a person gets older. As a result, cosmetics and medications designed to delay or slow down the aging process of the skin account for a sizeable portion of daily expenses for many individuals, particularly women.

This enormous aesthetic demand keeps the study of skin aging and its treatment going. Extrinsic and intrinsic variables both contribute to dermatological aging. Extrinsic aging is brought on by environmental factors like air pollution, smoking, poor nutrition, and direct sunlight exposure, resulting in coarse-textured wrinkles, decreased elasticity, inflexibility, and a rough-textured appearance. Intrinsic aging is an unavoidable biological process resulting in thin, dry skin, fine wrinkles, and progressive cutaneous atrophy. Remember that the main cause of extrinsic skin aging, also known as photoaging, is prolonged exposure to ultraviolet (UV) radiation from the sun. In this review, we will provide a summary of the alterations that occur as skin ages, as well as scientific developments on the molecular mechanisms causing these alterations and therapeutic options (Zhang, 2018).

Intrinsic Aging

The regular degeneration of skin brought on by chronological age and cyclical natural processes is typically referred to as intrinsic aging. When a person ages naturally, their skin thins down, wrinkles appear, and their skin gets coarser and more unusually dry. These innate attributes are personal traits that are not influenced by their surroundings. Therefore, fine wrinkles, dryness, and laxity are clinical features that characterize intrinsic skin aging. Other intrinsic characteristics include those related to gender, race, and anatomical differences. According to studies, the type, consistency, and susceptibility to environmental influences of aging skin vary between males and females. Age differences between people of various backgrounds have also been observed (Caturla, 2021).

I will go into more detail on how gender and life stages impact intrinsic aging below:

- ❖ **Gender and life stages**: Hormones and gender-specific variables may also be significant contributors to skin health and aging, depending on the individual's stage of life. For instance, men's lower eyelids have higher levels of sebum, skin pigmentation and thickness, deeper face creases, and more noticeable facial drooping. The earliest indications of aging start to show up around age 25. In fact, from this age forward, collagen synthesis declines by 1% per year. Following menopause, there is also a gradual loss of collagen content and a decrease in skin thickness, with annual losses of 2.1% and 1.1%, respectively. Given that estrogen insufficiency after menopause causes atrophic changes in the skin and rapid skin aging, this shows estrogen may have protective effects against skin aging (Caturla, 2021).

Extrinsic Aging

Skin aging is significantly influenced by environmental exposures, ways of life, and habits, with up to 85% of the visible indications of age directly attributable to external factors. Skin aging has been linked to a number of variables, including exposure to pollution and sunlight, smoking, poor nutrition, exercise, and excessive stress. The effects of smoking, sun exposure, excessive stress, and weight gain on aging have been demonstrated in studies using identical twins. An external sign of aging skin is uneven and erratic pigmentation, liver spots, and deep creases (Caturla, 2021). The effects of photoaging, pollution, and climate on extrinsic aging are explained below:

- ❖ **Photoaging**: Long wavelength, low energy infrared radiation (IRA), as well as visible light (VL) and ultraviolet radiation (UVR) with shorter, higher energies, are all components of sunlight. These pierce the skin at various depths. Long-wavelength UVA-1 rays are particularly significant because they thoroughly enter the skin and have noticeable effects on dermal fibroblasts. UVR, which includes UVA and UVB, is the main extrinsic factor affecting skin physiology.

❖ **Pollution**. The toxicological effects of air pollution on human health have become a prominent issue in recent years. In addition to UVR, experts have discovered that regular exposure to pollutants like polycyclic aromatic hydrocarbons (PAHs), volatile organic compounds (VOCs), oxides, particulate matter (PM), and ozone (O3) accelerates extrinsic aging and exacerbates inflammatory skin conditions like atopic dermatitis, eczema, psoriasis, acne, etc. In addition, new research suggests that the impacts of UVR and air pollution are interdependent and that the interaction between UVR and air-related traffic exhaust particles results in face lentigines.

❖ **Climate**. The look and texture of the skin are significantly influenced by seasonal changes. For instance, one study found that wrinkles and pigmentation were lessened in the winter compared to the summer, but moisture and the skin barrier decreased. Seasonal fluctuations affect skin hydration, sebum production, scaliness, brightness, and elasticity (Caturla, 2021).

Epigenetics and Aging

Even though the reasons for aging are not well understood, research is still being done to identify longevity pathways that are shared by all living things. Numerous studies that have successfully characterized the cellular and molecular signs of aging in recent years have made considerable gains. Among these signs of aging, epigenetic changes are a significant factor in age-related illnesses and the deterioration of cellular activities that it causes. By definition, epigenetics refers to transmissible processes that are reversible and don't involve changing the underlying DNA sequence. Although our genome's chromosomes contain genetic information, the epigenome is in charge of ensuring its stability and functional utilization; in other words, it links the genotype to the phenotype. These epigenetic alterations may occur on their own or be triggered by internal or external factors. The difference in aging patterns between genetically identical humans, such as identical twins, or between genetically identical species, such as queen and worker bees, in the animal kingdom may be explained by epigenetics. The majority of the remaining variance is believed to have developed through epigenetic drift over the course of their lifetimes, despite longevity studies on the human population showing that genetic variables can only account for 20 to 30% of the variations in life durations of monozygotic twins. Although queen and worker honeybees have the same amount of DNA, many environmental factors, including nutrition, produce significant modifications of stored epigenetic information, resulting in a remarkable variation in their physical features, reproductive activity, and mortality. Consequently, transcriptional drift and genomic instability are caused by the variation in the pattern of epigenetic information that develops as a population age within individual cells. Epigenetic information is established by enzymes and is reversible. Therefore, unlike genetic alterations, which are now theoretically irreversible in humans, epigenetics holds considerable promise for therapeutic intervention. Therefore, defining and comprehending the epigenetic changes that occur as we age is a significant field of current research that may eventually pave the way for the creation of innovative treatment strategies to prevent aging and age-related illnesses (Pal, 2016).

Key Takeaway Points

> Aging is a sequence of physiological modifications that affect a person's capacity to adapt to metabolic stress as well as biological functioning.

> The gradual development of both functional and structural modifications in an individual over time is referred to as the aging process.

> The changes manifest as a decline in fertility and physiological capacity from the person's peak age till death.

> Chronological aging. The years from birth to the present day are a person's chronological age. Your age is measured in years, months, days, and so on. The most typical way to establish your age.

> Biological aging. The gradual loss of a person's physiological capacity to satisfy demands over time is referred to as biological aging. The fundamental tenet

of biological aging is that your body's various cells and tissues get damaged as you age. In contrast to chronological age, which only takes into account the date of birth, biological age, sometimes referred to as physiological or functional age, takes into account several other factors.

➢ Psychological aging. Psychological age is different from chronological age in that it pertains to how old a person feels, behaves, and acts. If a person is mature or at least believes themselves to be older than they are, their psychological age may be larger than their chronological age.

➢ Social aging. The concept of "social aging" describes how society shapes our understanding of and experiences with aging. Social aging includes everyone's expectations and presumptions about how we ought to behave, what we are like, what we are capable of, and what we ought to be doing at certain ages (Shrestha, 2022).

Now that I've broken out the process of aging for you and the numerous components that influence it. It is now time to examine in the next chapter how humankind's different technological discoveries have influenced aging and laid out the road towards longevity.

Chapter 3

How Technology Is Reshaping the Future of Longevity

The Longevity Society and the Revolution of Technology

Thanks to modern technologies, older people can profit from staying put and maintaining relationships with loved ones. In a broader sense, it may support the development of inclusive work and living environments that enable older individuals to enjoy healthy and fulfilling lives. Longer term, advancements in technology, enhanced analytics, and a better knowledge of aging biology and human behavior will change the focus of therapy from curing disease to preventing it and promoting health (Dzau, 2021).

Humanizing technology to make it easier to age happily and healthily will be the biggest step forward for lifespan and health. This will result from a combined effort between people and machines. Healthcare practitioners will be able to generate precise diagnoses, individualized treatment, tailored health management, and efficient monitoring without having to visit the hospital thanks to advanced sensors, health data, and AI algorithms. You'll be taken to the hospital, and there will be care everywhere. The design of multichannel health delivery will be centered on the individual, giving them more autonomy and self-awareness to manage the behaviors, decisions, and lifestyles that result in an all-encompassing state of health (Hashmi, 2021).

Different Technological Advancements Developed Over the Years That Have a Strong Impact on the Longevity of Humans

The capacity of older people to live freely and self-sufficiently and fully enjoy their human rights on an equal footing with others has a great deal of potential to be increased via the employment of technologies like assistive technology and care robots. Robots and monitoring technologies might lessen elder abuse and mistreatment in care facilities and provide us with greater health-related information (Hicks, 2021).

Robotic care

In Japan, there are various robots that can provide companionship or household assistance to elderly people. Alzheimer's patients have been shown to get calming effects from Paro, the robot seal. The autonomous robot Asimo from Honda is capable of carrying out simple tasks like turning on and off lights or preparing meals for an elderly person. Although it doesn't really resemble a robot, Panasonic's Resyone carebot has received a distinction for being the first robot to satisfy ISO service robotics criteria. In actuality, it is a flexible object that may transform into a bed, chair, or motorized wheelchair as necessary. The Robobear robot is being created by RIKEN, a research facility in Japan, to carry people securely if necessary. Even robotic cats are available for those who can take care of themselves but still want a pet and company. Socially helpful robots for companionship and supported exercise are being tested on elderly individuals in the United States at USC's Human-Robot Interaction Laboratory. At the same time, IBM is collaborating with Rice University in the US to create a robot that can be a secure alternative to a human caretaker. The Multi-Purpose Eldercare Robot Assistant, or MERA, will be equipped with sensors that can recognize changes in older individuals' surroundings, behavior, and facial expressions. It will be able to detect whether someone has turned on the stove by accident, has fallen and needs aid, or is ill and requires medical attention. Although IBM is currently working on this robot and wants to make sure that each caregiver robot has all the knowledge necessary to help an elderly person, it is reasonable to predict that these robots may become prevalent over the next few decades. Information technology has new applications. Many industries have been transformed by modern technology, yet the sector of care for the elderly is often low-tech. The use of information technology by businesses like Honor Technology and HomeHero Inc. to connect caregivers with people in need of care might soon change that. To make sure that any full- or part-time caregiver is a good fit for the individual in need of care, both firms have developed sophisticated algorithms that are often updated. A caregiver's schedule, languages spoken, talents, and personality are taken into consideration. For family members and children of elderly parents who urgently want a short-term caretaker, Honor offers a service akin to Uber.

Smart Homes

The creation of smart houses and gadgets is another way that contemporary technology could influence senior care. An elderly person may rely on different technologies in the house to take care of duties that they are no longer able to complete alone rather than having a robot manage everyday chores like cooking, cleaning, and shopping. For instance, a smart refrigerator may detect when there is not enough food and place an order for supplies from a nearby supermarket or grocery shop. An older person can find it simple to allow in a family member or reliable caregiver without getting up and opening the door by using an app that is connected to a door lock system. There are already surveillance systems that can be placed in a home to enable friends and family to periodically check in on an elderly individual remotely; such systems are simple to operate with a smartphone to facilitate a grown child's checking in on what either parent is up to at any given time and guarantee that their elderly parents are secure and being cared for appropriately. Video calling systems are merely a step up from current home security camera systems and can be used by family members who wish to speak with elderly relatives, medical professionals who must counsel senior citizens on medication and health issues, and caregivers who wish to diagnose patients remotely so that doctors can promptly provide appropriate care (How Technology Will Impact Aging Now and the Near Future, 2023).

Artificial intelligence (AI)

The use of algorithms and artificial intelligence in the identification, diagnosis, and management of disease has become a crucial area of the biological sciences. Some people have called it the biggest healthcare revolution of the twenty-first century. AI may be able to identify diseases earlier and more accurately than conventional approaches. There is no longer a need for biopsies since AI is making it feasible to interpret mammograms for breast cancer 30 times faster and with virtually 100% accuracy.

Smart Bandages

Researchers in the United States have created a bandage that incorporates sensors to track the healing of wounds. According to the Stanford University team that developed it, it accelerates the healing of wounds, boosts fresh blood supply to damaged tissue, and improves skin regeneration by drastically lowering scar formation. A tiny electrical layer on the bandage has temperature sensors incorporated into it that monitor a wound's temperature. If more electrical stimulation is required to accelerate tissue closure, they can start that as well (Ellerbeck, 2023).

Key Takeaway Points

> ➤ The largest advance in longevity and health will come from humanizing technology to make it simpler to age contentedly and healthily.

> ➤ Technology developments like robotic care, artificial intelligence, smart houses, and smart bandages are just a few examples that contribute to longevity in humans.

All of the material I have provided in the previous chapters was intended to provide you all with a clear and succinct grasp of the human body and aging. I have now given you access to information that offers an in-depth look at certain contributing elements to longevity. My book's major goal—getting you to master the three infinite zones—will now be covered in Part 2.

Part 2

MASTERING YOUR 3 INFINITY ZONES IS AS EASY AS A.B.C.

Chapter 4

Infinity Zone 1—Anima

I want you all to learn how to harness the powers of the first infinity zone. My objective is to impart skills, resources, and methods that will enable each of you to maintain mental and emotional balance and vigor. The Latin words for "soul" and "spirit," anima and animus, respectively, were once employed to refer to the innately anti-sexual patterns in the collective subconscious. Men have an unconscious feminine image called the anima, whereas women have an unconscious male image called the animus. The idea of the mind being in balance is similar to the biological idea of homeostasis. As a result, while males have a mostly masculine consciousness, they require a feminine component in their unconscious to maintain a balanced psyche. For women, on the other hand, a compensating masculine element is required in their unconscious to maintain the equilibrium of their psyche because their consciousness is feminine. So, it makes sense that harnessing these archetypal energies is essential for psychological growth (Merchant, 2016). Philosophers, mystics, and scientists have pondered the underlying nature of life as well as the substance of the human experience throughout history. The idea of the soul, an elusive, illusory thing that is frequently connected to our innermost feelings, mental processes, and consciousness, has fascinated and baffled minds for centuries. I'll dive into the concept of infinity, looking at how it links to the soul of a person and why there can't be a multitude of infinities. The idea of the soul has been present in many spiritual and religious traditions, with each providing its own interpretation of this perplexing idea. Despite variances in culture and religion, a unifying theme emerges: The soul is frequently referred to as a non-physical, everlasting, and indivisible substance that forms the center of our existence. The soul is thought to be everlasting and unchanging, in contrast to our physical bodies, which are transitory and prone to change. The constraints of the physical world are transcended by the soul since it has no form or shape. It lives beyond time and space and is not constrained by them. This formlessness enables the soul to interact with others and the cosmos as a whole, weaving a complex web of connectivity. The principle of oneness and interconnectedness is the foundation for the notion that every person has one soul. Think of the entire universe as a huge ocean and each individual soul as a drop of water. Even though each drop seems unique, they are all made of the same substance: water. The soul is the commonality that unites all people, despite the fact that each one of us may appear to be unique. Since it has no beginning or end, infinity contradicts the idea of diversity. There would be a hierarchy of infinities if there were numerous infinities since one would definitely transcend the others. This, however, runs counter to the fundamental character of the infinite. So there can only be one infinity, which includes the infinite essence of the soul and all other facets of existence (Rai, 2023).

The Infinite Potential of Your Anima

People may not be aware of how closely the mind and body are related. Depending on a number of variables, they can have both positive and negative effects on each other. The mind-body link may be a concept you've heard before, but what does it actually entail? Researchers have discovered a remarkable link between our physical and mental well-being, suggesting that we may have more control over our bodies than we realize. Research has demonstrated that factors such as heart health, stroke risk, and other illnesses that were traditionally attributed to outside influences can have a significant impact on our psychological health. Stress is one of the main mental health issues that can cause physical symptoms. You might experience chronic stress in addition to headaches and a long to-do list. In fact, a 40% higher risk of acquiring or passing away from heart disease has been linked to people who endure chronic stress. Fortunately, there are many actions you can take to enhance your mental health, which will also benefit your physical health. Short-term mental health concerns can affect a person's symptoms, but long-term, untreated mental health problems can also affect a person's lifespan. Numerous studies have revealed that people with mental health conditions, including schizophrenia and depression, are frequently predicted to have shorter lifetimes. This frequently has to do with cardiovascular problems that grow with time. So what are some things you may do to live longer and be in better mental health? (*Healthy Heart, Healthy Mind*, 2023).

I have included a few techniques below that you may use to improve your mental health, for example:

1 **Focus on your cardiovascular health**: Heart and brain health are inextricably intertwined. Brain damage and cell death can result from poor blood flow and limited blood flow to the brain. If you take better care of your cardiovascular system generally, you will also take better care of your brain and make sure it receives all the oxygen- and nutrient-rich blood it needs for maximum function:

   ❖ Consume a heart-healthy diet. The Mediterranean diet, the DASH diet, and plant-based diets (vegan and vegetarian) are a few well-researched eating plans that can improve your cardiovascular health and lower your risk of stroke.

   ❖ If you have high blood pressure, learn how to regulate it. A high likelihood of cognitive impairment in later years and poor neurological conditions are both substantially linked to unhealthy blood pressure levels.

2 **Cut back on alcohol**: Additionally, if you smoke, make an effort to quit. Take more naps. Rest is one of Heights' 10 pillars of brain care for a reason. Giving the brain a rest has been proven to increase attention, boost cognitive function, and even help with complicated problem-solving since your brain works hard all day. Find opportunities to mentally recharge throughout the day, especially after concentrating on anything cognitively taxing. Take a stroll outside. Try

some yoga or meditation. Or even better, rest. The benefits of sleep for brain health are enormous. Your brain repairs itself, gets rid of any toxins that may have accumulated over the day, and transfers knowledge from short-term to long-term memory when you sleep.

3 **Activate your brain**: By encouraging the development of new brain cells and neural connections, maintaining mental and social stimulation enhances brain function. Consider learning a new skill, preferably in a group. This can mean taking up a new team sport, attending a painting class, or enrolling in dance lessons. You'll improve your mood, minimize loneliness and social isolation, and improve your brain health (feeling disconnected from society is a risk factor for negative brain health).

4 **Spend a few minutes working out every day**: Exercise has been shown to activate every area of the brain, enhance cognition, and even enlarge the regions of the brain involved in learning and memory. An ideal amount of daily activity is 30 minutes. You don't have to spend all day at the gym to maintain a healthy brain—walking the dog, working in the yard, or playing with your kids all count.

5 **Take smart supplements**: Don't forget to spend money on brain-health vitamins. Researchers have discovered several ways that your nutrition supports (or undermines) the functioning of your brain, a field known as nutritional psychiatry. The following are well-known vitamins, minerals, and nutrients that

support ideal brain function across all critical domains of brain health (*What is brain health, and why is the brain important?* 2023):

- ❖ Vitamins C and E are examples of antioxidants.

- ❖ Minerals like chromium and zinc are necessary

- ❖ EPAs and DHAs from omega 3

- ❖ And a lot more

The Power of Positive Thinking

Whatever you're going through, maintaining a positive mindset may assist both your mental and physical health. According to studies, people who face challenging circumstances with optimism and positivism may have improvements in their vascular health and may experience a slower rate of disease progression. However, it's crucial to understand that positivity is not the same as the absence of negativity. You must actively practice positivity and mindfulness if you want to benefit from having an optimistic mentality ("Healthy Heart, Healthy Mind: Understanding the Connection Between Mental Health and Your Body", 2023). Studies show that some personality traits, such as optimism and pessimism, can have an effect on your health and well-being in a variety of ways. The upbeat attitude that stress management often involves is crucial for effective stress management. Additionally, good stress management has several positive effects on health. You may develop positive thinking abilities even if you tend to be gloomy.

Negative life conditions should not be ignored in order to maintain a positive outlook. Positive thinking means approaching difficult circumstances in a positive and proactive manner. You expect the best, not the worst, to occur. Self-talk is frequently the first step toward positive thinking. Self-talk is the constant internal communication that takes place. Positive or negative thoughts may come to mind automatically. Your self-talk has some elements of logic and reason. Other self-talk may be the product of inferences you draw based on a lack of information or anticipations sparked by preconceived conceptions of what could happen. If you think mostly negatively, you're more inclined to have a bad attitude toward life. If your thoughts are typically optimistic, you probably believe yourself to be an optimist or someone who practices positive thinking.

The Health Benefits of Positive Thinking

There is an ongoing study being done on the effects of optimism and positive thinking on health. Several health benefits of positive thinking include:

- ❖ increased longevity

- ❖ decreased depression rates

- ❖ lower levels of anxiety and discomfort

- ❖ greater ability to fend off infections

- ❖ improved physical and psychological health

- ❖ lower risk of mortality from heart disease and stroke and improved cardiovascular health

- ❖ decreased likelihood of dying from cancer

❖ decreased chance of dying from respiratory diseases

❖ reduced danger of infection-related mortality

❖ enhanced coping strategies for challenges and stressful circumstances.

Positivity makes it less difficult for you to navigate trying circumstances, which lessens the negative effects stress has on your body's health. Additionally, it's believed that upbeat and optimistic individuals have better lifestyles—they engage in more exercise, consume a healthier diet, and don't smoke or overindulge in alcohol.

Ways to Identify Negative Thinking

Not sure if your inner dialogue is constructive or destructive? Typical examples of unfavorable self-talk include:

❖ **Filtering**: You highlight the negative aspects of a situation while ignoring all of its positive aspects. For instance, you had a great day at work. You received kudos for working diligently and quickly to complete your tasks ahead of time. That evening, you chose to put your goal of producing even more work ahead of the praise you received.

❖ **Personalizing**: You promptly assume blame for everything bad that occurs. When your date night is canceled, for example, you could assume that your partner does not want to be with you.

❖ **Catastrophizing**: Even in the absence of evidence, you instantly assume the worst will happen. Your order is misplaced at the fast-food drive-through, and you immediately fear for the rest of your day.

❖ **Blaming**: You make an effort to lay the responsibility elsewhere, away from yourself. You make an effort to avoid accepting responsibility for your thoughts and feelings. Suggesting that you "should" do something. You make a list of everything you believe you should do, and when you don't, you become mad at yourself.

❖ **Magnifying**: Your attention is drawn to small issues.

❖ **Perfectionism**: Setting oneself up for failure by maintaining unattainable standards and striving for greater perfection.

❖ **Polarizing**: All that you see is either nice or negative. There is no room for compromise.

How to Focus on Positive Thinking

It is possible to change your negative thoughts into good ones. Although the process is simple, it does take time and practice since, after all, you're creating a new habit. The following tips might assist you in thinking and acting in a more positive and happy manner:

1 **Determine what needs to change**: Start by recognizing the aspects of your life that you now have negative thoughts about, such as your work, your commute, your future ambitions, or a specific relationship, if you desire to think more positively and be more optimistic. By concentrating on one subject, you may begin small and tackle it in a more

constructive manner. Instead of a negative, consider one that will help you manage your stress.

2   **Do a self-check**: Stop and analyze your thoughts sometimes during the day. Try to find a technique to make your thoughts seem more optimistic if you discover that they are primarily negative.

3   **Be humorous-minded**: Especially during trying moments, give yourself permission to grin or chuckle. Look for comedy in mundane events. Life is more enjoyable when you can laugh about it.

4   **Maintain a fit lifestyle**: Try to include 30 minutes of exercise into your schedule most days of the week. During the day, you may also divide it into 5- or 10-minute intervals. Exercise has the power to boost moods and reduce stress. Eat well to nourish both your body and mind. Get adequate rest. And acquire stress management skills.

5   **Be in the company of uplifting individuals**: Make sure the individuals you surround yourself with are upbeat, encouraging, and capable of providing insightful criticism. People who are negative might make you feel more stressed out and make you doubt your capacity to handle stress in healthy ways.

6   **Engage in constructive self-talk**: Don't say anything to yourself that you wouldn't say to someone else is a good place to start. Be kind and supportive of yourself. When a negative idea arises, analyze it logically and counter it by focusing on your positive traits. Think

about the aspects of your life that you are appreciative of.

If you are more pessimistic than optimistic, expecting things to change overnight is impractical. But with time, you can learn to become less critical of yourself and more accepting of who you are. Always remember to be patient with yourself. You will eventually start to lose your sense of self-criticism. Being usually upbeat makes it easier for you to deal with everyday anxiety. That skill could help explain why positive thinking has been linked to several health advantages ("Positive thinking: Stop negative self-talk to reduce stress," 2022).

Engage in Gratitude and Mindfulness Exercises

❖ **Gratitude**: An excellent way to balance your emotions during difficult times is to practice appreciation. Even in the worst circumstances, there is always something to be thankful for. Keep a gratitude notebook or write letters to friends to document your thoughts of appreciation. Another benefit of gratitude is that it gets simpler the more you apply it, which leads to more regular feelings of happiness.

❖ **Mindfulness**: As we've seen, the way our bodies feel may be significantly influenced by the state of our brains. A technique to manage uncontrollable thoughts or sentiments that might harm our body and help keep them in check is mindfulness. Practices like breathing exercises, tai chi, and meditation may all help us calm down our thoughts and re-establish our connection to our bodies.

Since the heart and the mind are intertwined, both must be in good condition for there to be a healthy heart. Therapy is a fantastic way to reclaim your mental and physical wellness if you're struggling with mental health concerns or finding it hard to discover the good in life ("Healthy Heart, Healthy Mind: Understanding the Connection Between Mental Health and Your Body", 2023).

A List of Gratitude Exercises

1 **Journaling**: One of the simplest and most well-liked activities is to list a few things for which you are grateful. The activity asks you to think back on the previous day, a few days, or weeks and recall three to five things for which you are very thankful. By doing so, you are emphasizing all the positive events that occurred to you during a specific period.

2 **Gratitude reflection**: Reflection is a crucial component of mindfulness meditation and the development of self-awareness. A greater sense of wellness can result from these behaviors, among other advantages, but for most of us, a greater sense of well-being is enough of an advantage. The actions below might help you reflect on your thankfulness:

❖ Set yourself up in a calm position. To unwind and find your center, take a few deep, relaxing breaths. Let your focus shift to your immediate surroundings, including everything you can see, hear, taste, touch, and smell. Say to yourself, "I am grateful for this."

❖ Next, consider the individuals in your life that you are close to, such as your friends, family, and spouse. Say, "I'm grateful for this," to yourself.

❖ Next, focus on you. You are a special person with the capacity for communication, inventiveness, learning from the past to inform the present, and overcoming any suffering you may be going through. Say to yourself, "I am grateful for this."

❖ Let yourself finally relax in the knowledge that life is a priceless gift. That you were blessed with good health, a sophisticated upbringing, and access to spiritual guidance. That you were born during a time of extraordinary affluence. Tell yourself, "I'm grateful for this."

3 **Collage**: Similar to the thankfulness diary, with the exception that you'll be taking images of all the things you have to be thankful for. You may now picture yourself being grateful because of this. Consider documenting one thing for which you are thankful with a photo each day for a week. Consider your feelings. Examine the photos from the past week. It's not necessary to discover lofty reasons to be thankful. Any image of a flower will do. The more often you do this, the simpler it will be for you to identify the things for which you are thankful. You won't take these little

things for granted anymore. Maybe you'll take several images throughout the day to document. Put all of your photos in a collage after a certain amount of time has passed, and then just be thankful for what you have (Oppland, 2017).

List of Mindfulness Exercises

1 **Mindful seeing**: Anyone who can relate to this could find the practice of attentive seeing beneficial. It is a straightforward activity that simply needs a window with some sort of view. Follow these steps:

> ❖ Step 1: Locate a seat at a window where you can observe the outside world.

> ❖ Step 2: Observe all that is available. Avoid classifying and identifying what you see outside the window; rather than seeing a "bird" or "stop sign," try to focus on the colors, patterns, or textures that are present.

> ❖ Step 3: Pay attention to how the grass or leaves move in the wind. Take note of the numerous distinct forms that exist in this little area of the visible universe. Consider looking out the window, as someone unfamiliar with these things might.

> ❖ Step 4: Observe, but do not criticize. Observe it , but don't focus on it.

> ❖ Step 5: If you find yourself becoming sidetracked, gently nudge those ideas out of

your mind and focus your attention once again on a color or form to get you back on track.

2 **The five senses exercise**: With the help of this activity, you can easily practice mindfulness in almost any circumstance. All you have to do is pay attention to whatever you are experiencing with each of your five senses. Follow this order to practice the Five Senses:

❖ Notice five things that you can see. Focus on the five items you can see by taking a look at yourself. Pick something that you often overlook, such as a shadow or a tiny concrete fracture.

❖ Notice four things that you can feel. Bring your attention to four sensations you are now experiencing, such as the smoothness of a table you are resting your hands on, the texture of your jeans, or the sensation of the wind on your skin.

❖ Notice three things you can hear. Listen carefully for a moment and make a note of three background sounds. This might be a neighboring road's mild traffic noises, a bird's chirp, the refrigerator's hum, or other sounds.

❖ Notice two things you can smell. Bring your consciousness to odors, whether they are pleasant or unpleasant, that you often ignore. If you're outside, the air may be carrying the scent of pine trees or the odor of the fast-food outlet across the street.

❖ Notice one thing you can taste. Concentrate on a single flavor that is now available to you. You can detect the flavor that is now in your mouth by taking a sip of a beverage, chewing on some gum, eating anything, or even just opening your mouth and sniffing the air. This practice can help you rapidly enter a state of mindfulness and is rather simple. (Ackerman, 2017)

Unlocking the Anima Infinity Zone

With an emphasis on health span, I will examine the connection between mental health and lifespan. This section will discuss how to access your Anima Infinity Zone:

1. Relaxation techniques and stress management. Numerous health advantages have been linked to the use of relaxation practices, including meditation, prayer, and purposeful relaxation. These methods can aid people in managing stress, lowering anxiety and depression, and enhancing their general mental health. Studies have shown that using relaxation techniques can also have a positive impact on one's physical health, such as lowering blood pressure and boosting immunity. Stress is a typical event that may have an effect on a person's physical and mental well-being. Numerous chronic illnesses, such as depression, diabetes, and cardiovascular disease, can all be accelerated by prolonged stress. However, if you make

it a practice to use relaxation techniques, your ability to handle stress will improve, and stress levels will decrease.

2   Optimism, and a sense of purpose. Other crucial elements of mental health that might affect lifespan are optimism and a sense of purpose. Being optimistic means, you think good things may happen and that everything will turn out okay in the end. According to research, optimism is linked to a host of health advantages, such as improved immunological function, a decreased risk of cardiovascular disease, and reduced rates of depression. Similar to this, finding meaning or purpose in life may have an effect on one's mental and physical health. There is less melancholy and anxiety, better sleep, and a decreased risk of death in those who report having a sense of purpose in life, according to studies.

3   Engagement in mentally stimulating activities. Reading, figuring out puzzles, and acquiring new skills are all examples of cognitively stimulating activities that are linked to improved mental health and cognitive performance. According to studies, those who participate in cognitively challenging activities are less likely to experience cognitive decline and dementia. The same research has demonstrated that multilingual people have a higher cognitive function and a decreased risk of cognitive decline. To boost your mental health, practice engaging in cognitively stimulating activities. For instance, one study discovered that older people who participated in

cognitively engaging activities had a decreased incidence of depression.

A vital aspect of total health, mental health can affect both longevity and health span. A number of variables can enhance mental health and lower the risk of age-related disorders, including relaxation methods, stress management, optimism, a sense of purpose, and participation in cognitively challenging activities. These elements may affect the symptoms of aging, such as loss of proteostasis, cellular senescence, and mitochondrial malfunction. Therefore, encouraging mental health and taking part in mental health-improving activities may help people live longer, better lives (The Mind-Body Connection: How Mental Health Impacts Longevity and Quality of Life, 2023).

Additional Ways to Nourish Your Soul

Adopting good habits today can help nurture your soul, your thoughts, and your body more effectively than waiting until you reach a point when you start feeling trapped. Not only may it assist you in getting out of difficult situations, but everyday soul nourishment will also enable you to make life simpler for yourself.

Here are some ways to feed your soul:

1. **Do a healthy purge**: An excellent way to feed your soul is to let go of anything that no longer has value for you physically, emotionally, or spiritually. You will still have the people and things in your life that provide you with the most joy, love, and support. Here are some places to start where getting rid of some of the clutter could be beneficial:

- ❖ Unfit or out-of-date clothing that you haven't worn in over a year.

- ❖ People you know or have friends with who aren't loving, caring, or supportive of you.

- ❖ Your joyful, healthy existence is being hampered by food, drugs, or alcohol.

- ❖ Information and documents that you won't need and are merely collecting dust.

2   **Just breathe**: Our bodies naturally do this, but in this instance, I'm talking about intentionally breathing to experience several physical and mental advantages. Your immune system is bolstered, your muscles grow, and toxins are released as you breathe. You may focus better, feel less anxious, and relax your muscles by practicing conscious breathing. However, there is a skill to breathing correctly, so you may benefit the most:

- ❖ Breathing in via the nose and exhaling through the mouth.

- ❖ Give your stomach room to grow.

- ❖ Before exhaling, hold your breath for at least three seconds. Repeat as often as necessary.

- ❖ Better feelings come from intentionally taking deep breaths.

3   **Spend some time outside**: Trees, flowers, grass, animals, and sunshine all aid in relaxation, stress relief, and a deep sense of nourishment. Nature also has

magnificent sights and fragrances. The beautiful thing is that wherever you go, there is some aspect of nature to be found (even maintaining a plant inside your home can help). There is a method for everyone, regardless of circumstance, to gain from it as well:

❖ *Sunbathing*: Whether you do it at the beach, in your garden, or via your bedroom window, sunbathing may help you unwind and let your problems drift away. You might feel better with as little as 5 to 20 minutes of sunshine every day. It also raises your vitamin levels.

❖ *Gardening*: Some individuals adore getting their hands dirty and connecting with nature. Start by maintaining a plant in your house or by planting a garden. Looking at it will immediately make you feel less worried.

❖ *Outdoor activities:* Take up hiking, swimming, skiing, canoeing, horseback riding, soccer, tai chi, or simply go for a stroll. Take advantage of nature by doing everything outside.

❖ *Wildlife Watching*: Whether it is birds, deer, or butterflies, taking in the sights and sounds of the natural world is an incredible way to unwind.

4 **Consume actual food**: Are you aware of the ingredients in processed foods? Can you correctly pronounce half of the ingredients in processed foods? Real food keeps you healthy and gives you energy. Consuming more fruits and vegetables won't ever

make you feel less confident about yourself, but continuing to consume processed meals will. Additionally, it will certainly be more difficult for you to lose weight, which may result in higher medical expenses. Real food should also be consumed by your body if you truly wish to nurture your soul:

❖ Consume fresh produce.

❖ Avoid sugar, with the exception of natural sugar from fruit.

❖ Drink extra water since it hydrates you, helps you flush out toxins, and makes you feel satiated for longer.

5 **Spend time with those who are supportive of you and make you happy**: Meet-ups and support groups are excellent, as are friends and family. Invite a friend to watch a hilarious movie with you, take a stroll with you, or just converse on the phone. These straightforward actions may significantly improve your mood. Most of the time, what we really want is to be understood and appreciated. Keep in touch with the individuals in your life who can help you with that. They are priceless and will always serve as a reminder of all the wonderful things about you. Also:

❖ Avoid those who won't stand by you.

❖ Spend your time with those who will make you feel protected rather than condemned.

❖ If you don't feel you have somebody to turn to for assistance, consider joining a support group.

❖ Take in a pet. While people may have flaws, a pet won't ever be critical of you and may be a wonderful source of joy, love, and company.

6 **Meditate**: It helps when we stop for a while and just be still, listen to our own thoughts, or even become as inattentive as we can. Your body, mind, and soul experience a quiet that gives you the freedom to just let things go. Even a brief period of meditation may be quite beneficial. You will feel better, more at ease, and more present if you meditate for a longer period of time and more frequently. Follow these meditation tips:

❖ Instead of concentrating on your thoughts, pay attention to your breathing.

❖ Allow your ideas to enter, and then permit them to depart effortlessly. Then, go back to concentrating on your breathing.

❖ Obtain a cozy position. As you sit, ensure that your back is straight.

❖ To guarantee that you can concentrate and unwind while you meditate, find a secure, peaceful area. Anywhere, including outside, is possible (Kero, 2023).

Debunking Myths

Although the risk of dementia rises with age, it's crucial to remember that the disease is not a necessary component of aging. Many people continue to think and act normally well into their 90s and beyond. I'll be dispelling fallacies about the aging brain:

Myth 1: Exercise and a healthy diet are helpful for the heart but not so much for the brain.

Truth: Your brain will benefit from whatever is beneficial for your heart. Maintaining a healthy weight, eating a balanced diet, and exercising often all have significant positive effects on the heart and brain. One explanation is that since the brain is a vascular organ, it is essential for healthy blood vessel walls and robust blood flow.

Myth 2: A strong supplement routine helps keep your mind fresh as you age.

Truth: Everyone requires vitamins and minerals to be healthy, including the gray matter, but bottles of supplements that promise to improve cognitive function aren't the solution.

Myth 3: Playing brain games can prevent mental degeneration.

Truth: Although there is little to no proof that known brain games may maintain or enhance brain function, they may be entertaining. There are other cognitively engaging hobbies. Nevertheless, that may keep you bright. According to scientists, maintaining social engagement and learning new skills are beneficial for an aging brain. The same is true for returning to things you formerly found difficult and helping in your community.

Myth 4: In hospitals, older people frequently experience momentary confusion, which is acceptable.

Truth: Delirium, an abrupt shift in mental and behavioral states, is a frequent problem among elderly hospital patients and can have a long-term effect on brain health. It has been related to deteriorating dementia, depression, and anxiety.

Myth 5: There is little connection between the way you think and your mood.

Truth: As you age, your brain health has an impact on your mental health. In fact, having good mental health—feeling good, functioning well, and handling difficulties in life—is linked to a lower risk of developing dementia, whereas having poor mental health—for example, feeling useless or pessimistic—can affect a person's capacity to reason and think, as well as their ability to interact with others and control their emotions. You can keep your brain in good shape by finding activities you love and participating in them, as well as upholding important connections with family and friends (Nania, 2020).

Exercise Your Brain With These Mind-Body Techniques to Boost Innovative Thinking, Memory, and Cognitive Ability

Although the brain engages in vigorous daily activity, some activities may enhance connectivity and function. Even though you are sleeping, your brain is still working. However, some activities can alter how the brain functions, which may enhance memory, mental power, or creative ability:

1 **Visualizing**: To convey information, visualization entails creating an image in the mind. The mental image might take the shape of still images or animated sequences. In your daily life, you may put visualization into practice. For instance, you may plan how you'll travel to and from the grocery store before you go shopping, as well as what you'll buy there. The secret is to vividly and precisely see the situations in your mind's eye.

2 **Playing games**: A great way to pass the time or engage in some social interaction is by playing card or board games. These exercises could be good for the brain as well.

3 **Playing memory card games**: Playing memory card games puts one's short-term recollection and pattern recognition skills to the test. They are an easy and enjoyable approach to getting the brain working and stimulating memory and pattern recognition regions.

4 **Practice crossword puzzles**: One well-liked pastime that may engage the brain is solving crossword puzzles.

5   **Practice and complete jigsaw puzzles**: Jigsaw puzzle completion may be a fun way to kill time and could be helpful for the brain. Many cognitive processes are stimulated by puzzles, including:

  ❖ thinking

  ❖ mental circling

  ❖ operative memory

  ❖ deductive reasoning

6   **Playing Sudoku**: Sudoku and other number puzzles may be enjoyable mental exercises. For certain people, it could also enhance cognitive function. The cognitive performance of adults between the ages of 50 and 93 was shown to be improved in those who did number puzzles more regularly.

7   **Playing chess**: Playing checkers regularly improves brain function.

8   **Playing video games**: Action, puzzle, and strategy video games, for example, may result in advancements in the following areas:

  ❖ focus

  ❖ solving issues

  ❖ thinking elasticity

9   **Learning new skills**: Developing new abilities involves the brain in several ways and might enhance brain activity. The memory function of older people was found to be improved by learning a new,

cognitively demanding hobby like quilting or photography.

10 **Increasing your vocabulary**: Increasing your vocabulary is an outstanding way to expand your knowledge while mentally stimulating yourself. A quick technique to expand your vocabulary is to read a book or watch a TV show and make a note of any terms you don't recognize. Following that, you might check the word's definition in a dictionary and consider sentences in which you might employ it.

11 **Learning a new language**: The connection between various brain regions is boosted and strengthened by bilingualism.

12 **Listening to music**: The act of listening to music you like stimulates and links several brain regions.

13 **Learning a musical instrument**: The brain's coordination-related regions are worked out when learning an instrument.

14 **Taking up an engaging hobby**: Developing a new activity may be mentally exciting and provide new mental challenges. Hobbies that call for flexibility or synchronization will make you use your motor abilities. These interests can include:

- ❖ knitting
- ❖ embroidery
- ❖ drawing
- ❖ painting

❖ dancing

15 **Dancing**: Rhythm- and balance-related brain regions may be activated during dance, which is a form of exercise.

16 **Engaging in sports**: Some sports demand a lot from you mentally and physically. Some call for a variety of cognitive abilities, like:

❖ extended concentration

❖ organizing

❖ juggling multiple tasks

❖ the capacity to quickly adjust to changing circumstances

17 **Practicing Tai Chi**: Tai chi is a kind of physical activity that incorporates rhythmic breathing, soft body motions, and meditation. It improves communication between various brain areas.

18 **Sleeping**: Sleep is essential for the body and the brain, even if it is not always an active activity. Despite the fact that many people sleep less than they should, the majority of adults require anywhere from seven to nine hours of sleep each night. It has been shown that sleep:

❖ increase memory recall

❖ lessen mental fatigue

❖ control metabolism

As a result, getting adequate sleep each night is crucial for sustaining a healthy brain (Johnson, 2023).

19 **Increase caffeine intake**: Your memory may benefit from the caffeine included in beverages like coffee or green tea.

20 **Eat dark chocolate**: Dark chocolate may help you remember things better. It may seem indulgent. When tested on their ability to remember spatial relationships, individuals who ate dark chocolate outperformed those who did not. The study's findings revealed that flavonoids from cocoa increased blood circulation to the brain (Johnson, 2019).

Key Takeaway Points

➢ The soul transcends the limitations of the physical world since it is formless and limitless, and its connection with everything else points to how interrelated everything is. Even though we may all be diverse people, we are all little specks in the great ocean of consciousness.

➢ The principle of oneness and interconnectedness is the foundation for the notion that every person has one soul (Rai, 2023).

➢ Longevity is greatly influenced by the connection between the mind and body. You may increase your lifespan by engaging in numerous activities that stimulate the brain and thinking positively.

➢ Effective brain training may be achieved through simple tasks that require active brain involvement.

Others are specific mental exercises designed to enhance memory, intellect, or creativity.

➢ Exercise can improve the brain's performance and strengthen the links between its various areas. This may protect the brain from degeneration brought on by aging.

➢ Various people will likely like different types of mental pursuits. It would be wise to try out a range of brain-training activities at first and then concentrate on the ones that make you feel the most content or pleased (Johnson, 2023).

➢ In order to live long and full lives, it is important to take care of your soul. As such, you should regularly practice deep breathing exercises, decluttering, and meditation.

Making Knowledge Infinite

"Life is not about finding our limitations; it's about finding our infinity."

– Herbie Hancock

As we saw in the introduction, the idea of infinity means a lot of things, and throughout this book, we're zoning in on how you can release your infinite potential to live a long and healthy life.

I'd like to take this opportunity to take this idea of infinity in an extra direction too: By expanding our wisdom and sharing it with others, we can make sure that this philosophy of unlocking infinity to master longevity is, in itself, infinite.

As long as we keep spreading ideas, they remain in the world long after we've left it. And that isn't something any one of us can do alone. It requires information to be passed from one person to the next: It requires a chain of people who are willing to help.

I'd like to invite you to be part of that chain and help more people access the knowledge they need to ensure a long and fulfilling life. And if you're starting to worry that this sounds like an awful lot of work, don't panic: You don't even need to leave your living room. A short review will do the trick.

> **By leaving a review of this book on Amazon, you'll show other people where they can find the keys that will help them unlock infinity and pave the way for a healthy mind and body for the remainder of their lives.**

Simply by talking about how this book has helped you and letting new readers know what they'll find inside, you'll show them where they can find the guidance they're looking for – and you'll be part of the chain that will make this knowledge live forever.

Thank you for your support. Spreading knowledge takes a community, and I'm so happy that you're a part of this one.

Chapter 5

Infinity Zone 2—Body

Modern society favors healthier aging. According to research, adopting healthy practices may keep you active and healthy well into your 60s, 70s, and beyond. A progressive loss of muscle, decreased energy, and sore joints are all effects of natural aging-related changes in the body. These adjustments can persuade people to sit more and exercise less. But doing so increases your chance of contracting illness, becoming disabled, or even passing away. Finding the physical activities that will support your continued health and mobility should be done in consultation with your doctor (*Can you lengthen your life?*, 2016).

No matter your age or how much junk food you eat, it's never too late to start repairing the harm a bad diet has done to you. That's the message from researchers who look at how the foods we eat impact how long we live and how likely we are to get sick. They have discovered that cutting back on highly processed meals that are heavy in salt, sugar, and other additives and replacing them with more nutrient-dense foods like fruits, vegetables, nuts, beans, lentils, seafood, and whole grains can have significant positive effects on one's health at any age. It is best to start as soon as possible. The largest increases in life expectancy come from adopting a balanced diet as early as possible. However, even those who put off changing their dietary habits until their middle years or later can still live longer. Even little adjustments, such as reducing your consumption of processed meats like ham and hot dogs and replacing your noon snack with a handful of almonds, may possibly add years to your life.

And it implies that even if you're in your 60s or older, even these very little dietary modifications might still have a significant positive impact. If changing your whole diet sounds like a difficult job, start off by introducing a few key foods to your diet, for example (O'Connor, 2022):

❖ Consume a handful of nuts each day.

❖ Increase your consumption of whole grains. Instead of white rice, use brown rice.

❖ Consume at least a cup of beans, lentils, or peas per day. Eat a burrito bowl with pinto or black beans; include chickpeas in your salad.

❖ Add nut butter (peanut butter or almond butter) to toast, porridge, or yogurt for breakfast.

Long-term illnesses have a detrimental effect on life expectancy, although this effect can be mitigated by regular exercise and a healthy diet.

Unlocking the Body Infinity Zone

Every one of us has limitless potential as humans. But frequently, we are unable to access it because of our own limitations in terms of ideas and notions of what is conceivable. We become mired in our own patterns of thinking, doing, and being and fail to recognize the vast array of opportunities that are out there just waiting for us (Bueno, 2023).

Every one of us has limitless potential as humans. But frequently, we are unable to access it because of our own limitations in terms of ideas and notions of what is conceivable. We become mired in our own patterns of thinking, doing, and being and fail to recognize the vast array of opportunities that are out there just waiting for us.

When it comes to gaining access to your second infinite zone, which involves utilizing the human body, exercise is essential, but avoid overdoing it since this can cause damage to your knees, hips, and joints, especially if you push through discomfort. The good news is that some activities and diets can encourage tissue to heal and renew on its own.

The following recommendations are for exercising to increase your lifespan and your body's overall health:

Every day, take a quick, hour-long walk. One hour of daily walking may easily be accomplished. Consider choosing a coffee shop or restaurant that is fifteen minutes from your place of employment and making it a point to visit there twice daily. On the weekends, you may do it by walking instead of driving.

Every other day for 30 to 40 minutes, plus two hours on the weekends, engage in a 30- to 40-minute ride, run, or swim. The easiest method to accomplish this aim is to have a road bike as well as a stationary bike. If you can, ride your bike outside; if not, use it in high gear on an exercise bike with a high magnetic resistance setting, which makes pedaling difficult and simulates an uphill climb. Ten minutes in, you ought to be perspiring. Go upward for at least ten to fifteen minutes if you're riding on the road. Every other day for roughly 40 minutes, and on the weekends for two hours, perform this. Running puts more strain on the joints than riding could, making cycling potentially healthier. An injury brought on by long-distance running may be less frequent than we might anticipate, according to long-term research that found no link between the activity and osteoarthritis in healthy older people. Although I would advise using a bicycle in the first instance, jogging is okay as long as the guidelines listed below are followed. Another great activity is swimming; however, research on its lifespan benefits has not been as thorough as that on running.

Use your muscles. Humans are a species that constantly employs a variety of muscles while walking, running, and climbing trees and hills. Nowadays, people buy food rather than grow it, use dishwashers and washing machines rather than washing dishes and clothing by hand, drive rather than walk, and pay professionals to handle even small household repairs rather than doing things themselves. All of the body's muscles need to be utilized often since they can only develop, maintain, or increase in strength in reaction to challenges. Leg soreness might result from ascending six flights of stairs quickly, especially if you haven't done it in a while. The ache is a sign that your muscles have been somewhat injured. When enough proteins are present, muscle damage causes "muscle satellite cells" to activate, which eventually results in muscular development. By completing simple, hard actions on a regular basis, muscles can be somewhat harmed and then regenerated. Of course, minor damage might develop into a serious injury if the weight-bearing activity is too strenuous or if you repeatedly hurt muscles or cartilage that are already inflamed. To prevent both acute injuries and the delayed, chronic damage that results from disregarding discomfort and continuing to place force on an injured joint, muscle training must be balanced (Longo, 2018).

Rejuvenating cells. As we age, cells reach a toxic condition called senescence that causes havoc throughout the body, persistent low-grade inflammation, and illness, which effectively accelerates biological aging. In 2009, researchers discovered that giving middle-aged mice tiny doses of the medication rapamycin, which blocks the activity of a crucial protein called Mammalian Target of Rapamycin (mTOR), extended their lifespans and maintained their health.

Clearing out old cells. Another viable path involves eliminating all senescent cells. More and more research in the laboratory utilizing so-called "senolytics"—drugs that kill senescent cells—in mice demonstrates general health gains and longer lifespans for the mice since they are not succumbing to illness. Senescent cell removal benefits humans as well. In a limited clinical experiment, patients with severe lung fibrosis reported improved overall function, including improvements in their walking speed and distance, after receiving senolytic medication. This, however, is just the tip of the iceberg. More senescent cells may arise as a result of diabetes, obesity, and some bacterial and viral infections. Additionally, senescent cells increase the lungs' susceptibility to COVID infection, and COVID increases the number of senescent cells. Senescent cells must be removed from aged mice in order for them to survive a COVID infection (The Elixir of Youth: Science Explains How Humans Can Live Longer, 2021).

If you wish to realize your limitless potential, it is imperative that you take care of yourself. Be sure to get enough sleep, eat healthfully, exercise frequently, and set aside time for activities that bring you joy. When you put self-care first, you build a solid foundation that enables you to face obstacles and pursue your objectives with vigor and passion (Bueno, 2023).

Science-Based Techniques to Increase Gut Bacteria

The kind of bacteria in your gut might vary depending on a variety of circumstances, notably the foods you eat. Eating a fresh, well-balanced diet is the best way to achieve intestinal health. Your gut is home to around 40 trillion microorganisms in your body. Your gut microbiome refers to all of them collectively, and they are essential for overall health.

However, specific kinds of bacteria in your intestines may potentially contribute to a number of diseases, including:

1 **Consume a wide variety of foods**: There are hundreds of different types of bacteria living in your intestines, and each one of them has a specific role in preserving health and meeting various nutritional

needs. A diverse microbiome is generally seen as advantageous. This is because more bacterial species may have greater positive effects on your health. A diversified microbiome might result from a diet that includes a variety of foods.

2 **Consume a lot of fruits, veggies, and legumes**: Fruits and vegetables are the best dietary sources for maintaining a healthy microbiome. They have a significant amount of indigestible fiber. But some bacteria in your stomach can break down fiber, which promotes the growth of those bacteria. The fiber content of beans and other legumes is also very high. Several high-fiber meals are beneficial to your gut bacteria, including:

- ❖ raspberries
- ❖ artichokes
- ❖ green peas
- ❖ broccoli
- ❖ chickpeas
- ❖ lentils
- ❖ beans
- ❖ whole grains
- ❖ bananas
- ❖ apples

A fruit and vegetable-rich diet was shown to inhibit the growth of several disease-causing germs, according to one study:

3   **Consume fermented food**: This process, known as fermentation, occurs in foods when yeast or bacteria break down the carbohydrates they contain. These are a few instances of fermented foods:

  ❖   yogurt

  ❖   kimchi

  ❖   sauerkraut

  ❖   kefir

  ❖   kombucha

  ❖   Tempeh

These foods are frequently high in lactobacilli, a type of bacterium that is good for your health. According to research, those who consume a lot of yogurts seem to have their intestines populated by more lactobacilli. Additionally, these people had lower levels of Enterobacteriaceae, a group of bacteria linked to chronic diseases and inflammation:

4   **Consume prebiotic food**: Prebiotics are food items that support the growth of beneficial bacteria in the gut and are present in many foods. The majority of them are complex carbs or fibers that human cells cannot digest. Instead, some gut bacterial species break them down and use the pieces as fuel. Prebiotics may also be discovered on their own and are found in

many fruits, vegetables, and entire grains. Starch resistance is another property of prebiotics. The microorganisms in the large intestine break down this form of starch since it cannot be metabolized in the small intestine.

5 **Eat polyphenol-rich foods**: Plant substances called polyphenols offer several health advantages, such as lowering blood pressure, inflammation, cholesterol levels, and oxidative stress. Normally, human cells do not metabolize polyphenols. Most polyphenols are not sufficiently absorbed, so they end up in the colon, where gut bacteria break them down. Several instances of meals high in polyphenols include (Robertson, 2023):

- ❖ cocoa and dark chocolate

- ❖ red wine

- ❖ grape skins

- ❖ green tea

- ❖ almonds

- ❖ onions

- ❖ blueberries

- ❖ broccoli

An In-Depth Look at How Alcohol Can Affect Your Body

I have outlined that avoiding alcohol abuse is key to a long lifespan because of the damaging effects it can have on your health. Don't get me wrong, though. There is nothing wrong with having a drink now and then; the issue is excessive and frequent drinking. I will go into great length on the psychological impacts of alcohol misuse as well as the long- and short-term effects. Alcohol can have both immediate impacts, such as decreased inhibitions, and long-term ones, including immune system deterioration. Although you might not immediately feel the effects of alcohol on your body, they begin as soon as you take a drink for the first time. If you drink, you have experienced some of the effects of alcohol, from the warm rush that starts to wear off swiftly to the unpleasant wine headache or the hangover that appears the next day. You might not be concerned about them because they don't last long, especially if you don't drink frequently. A lot of people believe that drinking a beer or a glass of wine once in a while at mealtimes or on special occasions is not particularly harmful. However, drinking alcohol in any quantity has the possibility of being harmful to your health. Although those who binge or drink extensively may experience negative health impacts more quickly, even those who consume alcohol in moderation face certain hazards. Over time, alcohol usage can start to negatively impact anyone's physical and mental health. If you drink frequently and have a habit of having more than one or two drinks when you do, the impacts may be more severe and obvious. I will go into detail on how alcohol can affect your body, brain, and emotional health.

Excessive drinking of alcohol has both long- and short-term effects, and I will be exploring both below:

Short-term Effects of Alcohol

Among the short-term effects you could experience when consuming alcohol (or right after) are:

- ❖ emotions of sleepiness or relaxation

- ❖ mood swings caused by exhilaration or giddiness

- ❖ diminished inhibitions

- ❖ impulsive actions

- ❖ slurred or sluggish speech

- ❖ nauseous and dizzy

- ❖ diarrhea

- ❖ hearing, vision, and perception alterations as a result of head pain

- ❖ lack of coordination issues with concentration or decision-making

- ❖ loss of awareness or memory problems (sometimes known as a "blackout")

After just one drink, some of these benefits, including decreased inhibitions or a relaxed attitude, could become apparent. After a few drinks, certain additional symptoms, such as loss of awareness or slurred speech, may appear. Effects of dehydration, such as nausea, headaches, and dizziness, might take a while to manifest and vary depending on what, how much, and if you also drink water. Even though these effects might not last for long, they are nevertheless significant. Impulsivity, lack of coordination, and mood swings can impair your judgment and conduct and have more severe consequences, such as contributing to mishaps, injuries, and judgments you will later regret.

Long-term Effects of Alcohol

Alcohol consumption can also have long-term effects that reach beyond your personal health and enjoyment. Regular alcohol use may have the following long-term effects:

- ❖ prolonged mood swings, including agitation and anxiety

- ❖ insomnia and other issues with sleep

- ❖ a compromised immune system, which might cause you to become ill more frequently

- ❖ alterations in libido and sexual performance

- ❖ modifications to appetite and weight

- ❖ memory and attention issues

- ❖ trouble concentrating on things

- ❖ more strife in romantic and familial relationships

Alcohol's Physical Effects on Your Body

The impact of alcohol on your body's systems and internal organs is broken out below:

1 **Damage to your endocrine and digestive glands**: Over time, excessive alcohol consumption may result in pancreatic inflammation and pancreatitis. Abdominal discomfort and digestive enzyme release can both be brought on by pancreatitis. Serious consequences and long-term diseases can result from pancreatitis.

2 **Inflammatory injury**: Alcohol is one of the toxic chemicals that your liver uses in the breakdown and elimination of your body. Alcohol abuse for a long period of time impedes this process. Additionally, it raises your chance of developing chronic liver inflammation and liver disease brought on by alcohol:

   ❖ A disorder called alcohol-related liver disease can be fatal and cause your body to accumulate poisons and waste. Cirrhosis, or chronic liver inflammation, can result in scarring. Your liver may suffer long-term harm from scar tissue.

3 **Issues with your sugar levels**: Your body's response to glucose and utilization of insulin are both regulated by the pancreas. You may have hypoglycemia, or low blood sugar if your pancreas and liver aren't functioning correctly because of pancreatitis or liver illness. Additionally, a malfunctioning pancreas may limit the amount of insulin your body can produce and use to consume sugar. Hyperglycemia, or excessive

sugar in the blood, can result from this. If your body lacks the capacity to effectively manage and control your blood sugar levels, the effects and consequences of diabetes might become more severe. If you have diabetes or hypoglycemia, experts advise staying away from heavy alcohol use.

4. **Damage to your central nervous system**: Alcohol impairs the brain-body connection, which results in slurred speech, a crucial indicator of drunkenness. This makes speech and coordination more difficult (think about balance and response time). This is why you should refrain from drinking and driving.

5. **Over time, alcohol could cause harm to your central nervous system**: Your hands and feet may start to feel tingly and numb. Additionally, drinking might impair your capacity for:

   ❖ make lasting memories

   ❖ mental clarity

   ❖ make logical decisions

   ❖ control your feelings

6. **Drinking over time can also harm your frontal lobe**: This is the area of the brain in charge of executive processes, including abstract thought, judgment, social conduct, and performance. Additionally, sustained excessive drinking can lead to lasting brain damage, such as Wernicke-Korsakoff syndrome, a memory-related brain condition.

7   **Digestive system problems**: The link between drinking alcohol and digestive health may not be immediately obvious. Often, the adverse effects don't show up until after the damage has been done. Drinking more can make these sensations worse. Drinking can harm the connective tissue in your digestive tract, making it difficult for your intestines to properly digest food and assimilate vitamins and nutrients. Malnutrition may result from this harm over time. Excessive drinking can result in:

- ❖ gas

- ❖ bloating

- ❖ sense of satiety in your stomach

- ❖ diarrhea or uncomfortable stools

- ❖ hemorrhoids or ulcers (caused by dehydration and constipation). Without timely identification and treatment, internal bleeding brought on by ulcers may occasionally result in death.

8   **Circulatory system problems**: Drinking excessively over time can harm your heart and lungs and increase your risk of heart-related illnesses. High blood pressure is one of the difficulties of the circulatory system. Other issues include:

- ❖ unsteady heartbeat

- ❖ blood circulation across the body is problematic

❖ stroke

❖ chest pain

❖ heart condition

❖ heart disease

❖ anemia, a disorder marked by a low red blood cell count, and exhaustion can be brought on by problems receiving vitamins and minerals from meals.

9 **Reproductive and sexual health issues**: You might imagine that since alcohol can lessen inhibitions, it would increase the amount of enjoyment you have in bed. However, excessive drinking can:

❖ stop the synthesis of sex hormones

❖ decrease libido

❖ prevent you from achieving or keeping an erection

❖ make it challenging to induce orgasm

❖ drinking too much might alter your menstrual cycle and perhaps raise your chance of infertility.

10 **Muscular and skeletal system damage**: Alcohol abuse over a long period of time can reduce bone density, making bones brittle and raising the possibility of fractures in the event of a fall. Weaker bones may also mend more slowly. Alcohol use can also result in

weakened, cramped, and eventually atrophying muscles.

11 **Immune system weakness**: Heavy drinking compromises your body's natural immune system. When your immune system is weak, it must work harder to protect you from viruses and germs. Long-term heavy drinkers are also more likely than the average population to get TB or pneumonia. Alcohol use can potentially raise your chances of developing cancer:

❖ Your chance of getting liver, colon, breast, esophageal, mouth, and throat cancers can all rise with frequent drinking.

❖ Your chance of acquiring mouth or throat cancer might be considerably increased if you also drink or smoke.

Alcohol Use During Pregnancy Is a Big NO!

Alcohol is not thought to be safe for expectant mothers. This is due to the fact that drinking while pregnant has effects other than your health. It could result in a stillbirth, miscarriage, or early delivery. After birth, newborns who were exposed to alcohol while still developing might develop a number of issues, such as:

❖ learning challenges

❖ persistent health problems

❖ heightened emotional issues

❖ development issues

Psychological Effects of Excessive Drinking

Alcohol abuse over a long period of time might alter your brain in ways that include:

- memory and attention span

- impulse management

- feelings, attitude, and personality

Habitual drinking can also hurt one's general psychological well-being, in part because it can make the symptoms of some mental health problems, such as depression, anxiety, and bipolar disorder, worse. While suffering from a hangover, you could experience anxiety. Issues with mental health brought on by alcohol. Alcohol consumption can contribute to symptoms of mental illness that closely mirror those of other mental health problems, such as:

- ❖ alcohol-induced bipolar disorder

- ❖ alcohol-induced psychotic disorder

- ❖ alcohol-induced sleep disorder

- ❖ alcohol-induced depressive disorder

- ❖ alcohol-induced anxiety disorder

You will only experience symptoms of these disorders during alcohol withdrawal or intoxication. Usually, these symptoms disappear shortly after stopping alcohol use. Some people end up becoming extremely dependent on alcohol. In fact, some drinkers gradually build up a tolerance to it. They gradually have to consume more to experience the same impacts they previously experienced.

Other psychological effects of alcohol include:

1 **Dependency**: Regular alcohol use can also result in dependency, which indicates that your body and brain are accustomed to the effects of alcohol. You could experience a variety of physiological, psychological, or mental health problems when you quit drinking, which go away as soon as you consume another drink. Both addiction and tolerance can be signs of alcohol use disorder, a condition that was formerly known as alcoholism and occurs when your body becomes reliant on alcohol. Based on the number of symptoms you have, this disease may be serious, moderate, or mild. Significant signs may include the following:

   ❖ urges

   ❖ withdrawal

   ❖ over time, increase in drinking

   ❖ having trouble cutting back after one drink

   ❖ inability to quit drinking despite efforts

   ❖ continuing to use alcohol despite its detrimental effects on your health or way of life

   ❖ taking a lot of time doing things linked to drinking

2 **Alcohol withdrawal**: Detoxification from alcohol can be challenging and, in extreme circumstances, fatal. Depending on how much and how often you drink, you might want assistance from a medical expert to stop. It is always advisable to speak with your doctor before stopping drinking. Going "cold turkey" may not always be a good idea. Acute withdrawal effects from alcohol include:

- ❖ anxiety

- ❖ nervousness

- ❖ nausea

- ❖ tremors

- ❖ high blood pressure

- ❖ unsteady heartbeat

- ❖ heavy perspiration

- ❖ Severe withdrawal might result in seizures, hallucinations, and delirium

You may stop drinking healthily with the aid of medical detoxification. Depending on the likelihood that you may have withdrawal symptoms, your doctor may advise therapy at home instead of at a clinic. Your chances of developing an alcohol consumption problem may be increased by specific circumstances. A few of these are:

- ❖ binge drinking

- ❖ excessive drinking

- ❖ continuing stress

- ❖ having relatives or friends that are heavy drinkers

- ❖ possessing genetics that influences alcohol susceptibility

- ❖ having a mental health issue such as anxiety, depression, schizophrenia, or another one

- ❖ having a parent or other close family member with the disease

Alcohol Safety Tips You Can Follow

Although there isn't a perfectly risk-free way to consume alcohol, these recommendations can help reduce some of the hazards (Raypole, 2023):

1 **Do not forget to eat**: To slow down the onset of intoxication, avoid consuming alcohol on an empty stomach.

2 **Drink a lot of water**: Make an effort to drink one glass of water for every alcoholic beverage you consume.

3 **Do not drink too fast**: Take slow, deliberate sips to give your body time to process the alcohol. Your liver may digest one ounce of alcohol per hour.

4 **Avoid combining alcohol with other drugs**: Caffeine may make alcohol's depressive effects less noticeable, causing you to drink more than you normally would. While drinking coffee to "sober up" may help you feel more alert, it might also increase your risk of driving while inebriated. Alcohol and

other substances used together might have negative effects.

5 **Avoid drinking and driving**: Never drive after drinking. Even if you feel like you've sobered up, you can still have alcohol in your system, which might cause a delay in your reaction time.

Debunking Myths

I need to dispel some myths regarding lifespan. Additionally, these may have been urban legends that many of you believed to be genuine, but I'm here to shed some light on that (Dolgoff, 2021):

Myth: Overworking yourself will result in premature death.

Truth: A hard worker's probability of dying young is 20% to 30% lower. It's detrimental to your health if your job causes take-home stress. But for the majority, employment has actual advantages due to the social interaction and cerebral stimulation it provides. The thing that promotes longevity, however, is not money so much as a feeling of purpose. Almost every endeavor may have a purpose, whether it's taking up a new social interest or volunteering to assist in caring for a grandchild.

Myth: You will experience early death if your family has a propensity for it.

Truth: Your longevity is only partially influenced by your genes. A parent who survives past the age of 70 increases the likelihood of living longer, so yes, your DNA does play a role in this. However, your surroundings and dietary choices, which influence how your DNA manifests itself, are considerably more important.

Myth: Aging is the worst thing ever!

Truth: This could not be further from the truth. People who welcome aging tend to live 7.5 years longer than those who fear it. This might be because people who are pessimistic about getting older are less likely to seek health care when problems arise; they may just attribute them to aging and neglect to treat them.

Myth: It's too late to change detrimental behaviors like smoking and tanning.

Truth: It is never too late to take steps to enhance your health and extend your life. People who quit smoking between the ages of 45 and 54 lived six years longer than those who continued to smoke. The same criteria apply to deciding to become more active.

Key Takeaway Points

➤ A diversified microbiome is good for your health and can result from consuming a varied diet high in whole foods.

➤ Numerous fruits and vegetables contain significant amounts of fiber. Fiber encourages the development of good gut bacteria, particularly particular varieties like Bifidobacteria.

➢ The microbiome can benefit from fermented foods like plain yogurt by improving its performance and lowering the number of disease-causing bacteria in the intestines.

➢ Prebiotics promote the growth of a range of beneficial bacteria, such as bifidobacteria. According to certain research, prebiotics may lower insulin, triglyceride, and cholesterol levels, lowering risk factors for specific medical diseases.

➢ Human cells are not very good at digesting polyphenols, but gut bacteria are quite good at doing so. They might enhance a number of heart disease- and inflammation-related health outcomes.

➢ In healthy individuals, probiotics do not dramatically alter the microbiome's makeup. However, in people with specific medical disorders, they may enhance microbiome activity and assist in restoring the microbiome to health (Robertson, 2023).

➢ Participating in different physical activities significantly lengthens your life and improves your general mental health.

Chapter 6

Infinity Zone 3—Community

All individuals, but notably older adults, have come to rely on social engagement for their overall health. How essential is social well-being, though? Starting off, social stimulation is good for your well-being since it makes you feel happy, improves your mood, lowers your risk of dementia thanks to the power of discussion, and fosters a sense of safety and community. Healthy sociability has the effect of enhancing overall wellness in older people ("Social Interaction and Longevity Amongst Seniors", 2022). One of the main advantages of social interaction is how it affects physical health, which is essential for maintaining a long and happy life.

Fostering close relationships with others and feeling a sense of being part of something has repeatedly been linked to a longer lifetime, mostly due to the following causes and impacts (Hetherington, 2023):

❖ **Improved health**: People who have supportive social networks are less likely to suffer from heart attacks, strokes, and other cardiovascular disorders. Increased immune system performance and lower inflammation, which are connected to chronic illnesses and faster aging, have both been linked to social interaction.

❖ **Improved practices**: Strong social ties can persuade individuals to engage in better habits like eating a balanced diet, seeing the doctor frequently, and abstaining from dangerous practices like smoking or binge drinking. In addition to providing encouragement and company, social relationships can promote physical fitness and general health by encouraging frequent activity.

❖ **Cognitive exercise**: Social interaction encourages mental flexibility, creativity, and problem-solving abilities. Social contacts promote intellectual discourse, expose us to fresh insights and information, improve cognitive health, and lengthen our lifespan.

❖ **Emotional health**: Social interactions reduce feelings of isolation and loneliness while fostering a sense of belonging and emotional health. A network of dependable connections can also offer emotional support during trying times, promoting general mental health, and extending life.

❖ **Enhanced compliance with medicinal treatments**: Social support can help patients adhere to medical therapies and treatments, which can enhance the management of chronic illnesses and the quality of life. According to several studies, those who have strong social support systems recover and heal more quickly from procedures, diseases, or traumatic experiences.

❖ **Life fulfillment and a sense of purpose**: Social relationships promote a sense of interconnection, purpose, and belonging, which in turn increases life pleasure. Participating in social networks offers a supportive group that improves general well-being and fosters a happy and purposeful existence.

❖ **Mental health and social connectedness**: In addition to being crucial for our physical health, social interaction has a significant impact on our mental health. Reduced stress and anxiety are only a couple of the psychological advantages that social interaction offers, which is why it is so important for improving mental health. Through understanding and empathy, social relationships provide a supportive network that can reduce stress and anxiety. By giving one a sense of comfort and certainty, having solid social ties may also aid in overcoming difficult circumstances.

❖ **Increased confidence and self-worth**: Social relationships offer acceptance and validation, which can raise one's self-esteem and confidence. In addition to providing criticism and encouragement, supportive partnerships foster personal development and boost self-confidence.

❖ **Enhanced resilience**: Social relationships are an invaluable tool for overcoming obstacles in life and getting access to other viewpoints and solutions. A sense of camaraderie and belonging that comes from being a part of a social network also helps to build resilience and advance mental health.

❖ **Enhanced mood and happiness**: A brighter and happier attitude towards life is facilitated by engaging in enjoyable social interactions, which foster good feelings and laughter. The happiness and connection that come from sharing experiences and pursuits with others also promote a positive mood.

Unlocking the Community Infinity Zone

The following tactics will help promote meaningful relationships and create a more rewarding and connected existence for those of you who are reading this and are trying to increase your social connections but are unsure of where to start:

❖ **Build and consolidate current connections**: Utilize the connections you already have by reaching out to friends, family, and other loved ones on a regular basis, doing things together, and sharing experiences. Deeper connections and stronger friendships are also fostered by actively listening and demonstrating empathy in conversations.

❖ **Broaden your social network**: Making new relationships can be facilitated by taking part in group activities, joining clubs or organizations, and volunteering for local issues or events. Attending social events or networking functions offers chances to connect with like-minded people and widen social networks.

❖ **Welcome technology**: Even when being close to loved ones is difficult, technology such as social networking platforms may help you keep in touch with them. You may meet new individuals and broaden your network by participating in online groups and forums with others who share your interests.

❖ **Overcome obstacles**: If you experience social anxiety, get support or professional assistance. Small moves outside your comfort zone, like striking up conversations or going to social events, might help you gain confidence over time. Therapy or support groups are excellent sources for overcoming social difficulties and learning practical techniques.

❖ **Develop meaningful relationships**: Stronger ties and a sense of belonging are nurtured by devoting time and effort to developing meaningful connections with people and expressing gratitude for their presence. In the end, developing meaningful relationships enhances our lives and adds to our overall health, happiness, and longevity.

❖ **Obtaining expert assistance**: For assistance with enhancing social skills or overcoming obstacles, talking to therapists or counselors can offer insightful advice and methods. Participating in support groups or group therapy for those with social issues can provide a safe setting where you can grow and learn from others' experiences.

Although it takes work and active participation to establish and sustain social ties, the benefits in the form of enhanced well-being and a fuller, more connected existence are well worth the expense (Hetherington, 2023).

Things to Keep in Mind

Even more of a health concern than cigarette smoking, being overweight, and leading a life of inactivity is loneliness. There are several reasons why loneliness raises the risk of heart disease, stroke, and death. One widely accepted theory is that people who are disconnected from society are more likely to indulge in unhealthy habits, including smoking, gaining weight, and drinking too much alcohol. Another theory is that the detrimental psychological conditions brought on by loneliness alter the body in ways that raise the danger of heart attack, stroke, and death. This involves a rise in the activity of the hypothalamic-pituitary-adrenal (HPA) and sympathetic nervous systems, two components of your stress response.

I want you to be cognizant that the cascading repercussions of loneliness include inflammation, high blood pressure, increased blood clotting, and reduced immunological function, all of which contribute to plaque formation in the arteries, which results in heart attack, stroke, and death. It's also not simply conjecture. In an extremely tangible way, loneliness and social exclusion are harmful to your health. I'm not trying to terrify any of you who are reading this; rather, I want to keep you informed and encourage you to make an effort, especially if you see that you are isolating yourself more than normal, since friendship is a wonderful remedy for this. Spending time with those you care about and forming new connections doesn't actually have any "side effects."

Having strong social ties raises your chance of surviving by 50% overall. According to one survey, more than 80% of centenarians maintain regular contact with friends or family.

Become active in your community as well. Research has shown that going to church frequently lowers the chance of organ failure and mortality. According to several studies, this is at least in part because people are more socially connected and have healthier habits. If you are not religious, it is conceivable that other social organizations and events might provide you with similar advantages. For thousands of individuals, Cross Fit, for instance, has acted as a meeting place. Meetups are yet another fantastic illustration of how to come together and engage socially with individuals who share your interests and ambitions. Find a club, sign up for a team, go to a funny lecture series, and then hang around for coffee afterward. Engage in social interaction and maintain your current friendships and family ties however you want to do it. Getting together with those who share your views and interests has a certain appeal (Doron, 2020). Give the Infinity Zone 3 method a try. It may even help you live longer.

Debunking Myths

I will be dispelling other longevity misconceptions that I believe will alter your perspective and offer many of you further knowledge and clarification:

> **Myth**: Only wealthy people can live longer

> **Truth**: While wealth and access to healthcare can influence lifespan, evidence indicates that socioeconomic position is not the main determinant. Dietary habits, physical activity, stress management, and supplements are all within most people's grasp and can have a

substantial influence on the length of time we live.

Myth: Strict commitment to a certain diet or fitness routine is necessary for longevity.

Truth: Perfectionism is not the aim when it comes to your life! According to research, no matter how modest or significant a change you make to your lifestyle habits, such as those related to your food, exercise, supplements, and stress management, it may still have an impact on how long you live and how healthy you are.

Myth: Longevity is a problem only for the elderly.

Truth: Individuals of all ages should strive for longevity. Early adoption of good lifestyle practices can improve your chances of living a longer, healthier life. Additionally, some illnesses that might shorten lifespans, such as heart disease and several types of cancer, may manifest earlier in life.

Myth: Red wine's component, resveratrol, is beneficial for longevity and can help you live longer if you drink it daily.

Truth: Red wine does contain substances that some claim to have health advantages, such as resveratrol; however, the amounts are really minuscule, and even higher amounts are dubious (*The 7 Biggest Longevity Myths*, 2023).

Key Takeaway Points

- Human well-being is critically dependent on social interaction, which affects both your physical and mental health.

- Strong social ties are associated with a longer lifespan than social isolation.

- You may invest in social interaction to benefit both your physical and psychological wellness as well as your sense of purpose in life (Hetherington, 2023).

Chapter 7

Putting Together the A.B.C. of Infinity

When it comes to unlocking the infinity zones, there is no universally applicable solution. Regardless of your age, you are all unique individuals with unique personalities, physical characteristics, and life experiences. As a result, your demands and routines will vary. You must design a customized routine that works with your lifestyle, your requirements, and your short- and long-term objectives. You all must first recognize who you are before using the procedures. You may choose the most effective routine to employ and adhere to by being self-aware. You must determine which tactic suits you best. Self-awareness is the capacity to reflect on and examine oneself critically. There are different levels of self-awareness, even if it may not be feasible to achieve complete objectivity regarding oneself—a controversy that has persisted throughout philosophy. It can be found on the spectrum. Although self-awareness is something that everyone understands in general, we don't entirely comprehend where it comes from, what its forebears were, or why some of us seem to have more or less than others.

We can just think, feel, and behave as we will throughout the day, not giving ourselves inherently any more consideration; yet, we can also direct our attention to that inner part of ourselves. We might consider if we are doing and feeling according to our norms and principles or as we "should" when we self-evaluate. This is referred to as measuring against our accuracy standards. We do this every day, employing these standards to assess the legitimacy of our beliefs and actions. To exercise self-control, it is important to use these criteria as we assess and decide if the decisions, we are making will help us attain our objectives (Ackerman, 2020). Because of this, you must develop self-awareness before coming up with a sustainability regimen. Making a longevity regimen that works for you will come naturally, and with time, it will become a part of your everyday routine.

Creating Your Longevity Plan

Want to live a longer, healthier, and more satisfying life? If this is the case, making a longevity strategy is the best method to accomplish your objectives. I'll coach you through the essential processes and techniques for developing a longevity plan in this in-depth manual, so you may live the life of your dreams. A tailored blueprint outlining the behaviors and habits you should develop in order to live a healthier, more productive, and more meaningful life is known as a longevity plan. It makes a strategy that is specifically suited to your requirements by taking into consideration a variety of variables, including your present health state, lifestyle decisions, and your genetic makeup. Because it enables you to take charge of your physical and mental well-being, a longevity plan is essential. You may greatly improve your probability of living a longer and happier life by taking preventative measures to address probable health concerns and forming healthy routines.

Key Steps in Creating Your Longevity Plan

* ❖ **Analyze your present state of health**: To determine your current health state, make an appointment for a thorough health checkup. This will aid in locating any underlying health problems that require attention. Consult with medical specialists, such as nutritionists and physicians, to seek recommendations on how to improve your overall wellness.

* ❖ **Make plans for an extended life**: Establish your objectives for a long life. What objectives do you have for your long-term strategy? Would you like to prolong your life, get healthier overall, or avoid certain diseases? To maximize your chances of success, develop SMART goals for your objectives: precise, measurable, attainable, pertinent, and time-bound.

* ❖ **Take up a fit lifestyle**: Consume a diet that is well-balanced and full of fresh produce, whole grains, lean meats, and healthy fats. Exercise regularly to maintain a healthy weight and to enhance your cardiovascular health, such as walking, running, swimming, or cycling. Sleep enough to let your body recover and regenerate. Utilize methods to reduce stress, including

deep breathing exercises, meditation, or indulging in enjoyable hobbies.

❖ **Preventative medicine**: Maintain current immunization and screening records to identify and stave off future health risks. Follow recommendations for blood pressure monitoring, cholesterol testing, cancer screenings, and other preventative procedures.

❖ **Control persistent circumstances**: Work closely with your medical team to properly manage and control any chronic diseases you may have, such as diabetes or hypertension. To keep track of your condition, take your medications as directed and schedule routine checkups.

❖ **Keep your mind and heart in good shape**: Try to find ways to keep your mind active, such as reading, solving puzzles, or picking up a new skill. Develop a solid social network and keep up your friend and family support system. If you are dealing with mental health problems like depression or anxiety, get expert assistance.

❖ **Routine health evaluation**: To track your development and make any required modifications to your longevity strategy, schedule frequent health examinations. To make sure you are on the proper path, monitor your health indicators like blood pressure, cholesterol, and body mass index (BMI).

❖ **Making a strategy for longevity is a proactive move toward living a longer, healthier, and more rewarding life**: You may take charge of your health and well-being by adhering to the essential procedures and ideas provided in this book. By developing your personal longevity plan, you may begin your path to a longer, better quality of life right away (*The Ultimate Guide to Creating a Longevity Plan for a Healthy and Fulfilling Life*, 2023).

Key Takeaway Points

➢ A customized blueprint outlining the behaviors and habits you should develop in order to live a longer, healthier, and more meaningful life is known as a longevity plan.

➢ Establish longevity objectives, lead a healthy lifestyle, take part in preventative care, manage chronic illnesses, maintain mental and emotional well-being, and routinely check your health ("The Ultimate Guide to Creating a Longevity Plan for a Healthy and Fulfilling Life," 2023).

Part 3

LEARNING FROM THOSE WHO LIVED THE LIFE

Chapter 8

Lessons From the Blue Zones—The Secrets of Long-Lived Communities

Likely, some of you have never heard of blue zones. It undoubtedly sounds like the name of an energy drink to some of you. Blue zones, however, have high rates of lifespan. Let's face it; nobody truly lives forever. However, the majority of you aim to live as long as you can. The impact of good habits can be significant (*What are Blue Zones?*, 2023).

The term "Blue Zones" refers to geographical locations with some of the oldest inhabitants in the world (Robertson, 2017). Each Blue Zone has its own way of life. They do, however, frequently share a few characteristics. For instance, the majority of the population in each area consumes plant-based foods. They eat a lot of veggies and beans and very little meat. And they abstain from overeating ("What are Blue Zones?" 2023).

Dan Buettner's National Geographic investigation into the mysteries of long life finally led to the discovery of the Blue Zones, five areas worldwide where people consistently live to be over 100 years old. The original goal of Blue Zones was to identify the best lifestyles that promote vitality and longevity. Twelve years after the big project's inception, Blue Zones is now a method for creating the healthiest lives for both people and entire communities. The objective of Blue Zones is to make healthy living not only simple but also an inevitable choice (Buettner, 2016).

Five Blue Zones That Have the Healthiest People

1 **Ikaria, Greece**: There are very few cases of dementia and middle-age mortality on this island in the Aegean Sea, which lies eight miles off the coast of Turkey. Their typical Mediterranean diet, which is high in vegetables and heart-healthy fats and low in dairy and meat, has been linked to a longer lifespan, according to research.

2 **Loma Linda, California**: Seventh-day Adventists make up the majority of the population in this area, and those who eat according to the Bible's recommended ratio of grains, fruits, nuts, and vegetables tend to live 10 years longer than the typical American.

3 **Nicoya Peninsula, Costa Rica**: There are the fewest middle-aged deaths worldwide and the second-highest number of male centenarians in this region of Central America. Their strong religious groups, extensive

social networks, and routine low-intensity physical exercise routines are some of the reasons they live so long.

4 **Okinawa, Japan**: The longest-living women in the world reside in Okinawa, the biggest island in a subtropical group that Japan controls. Okinawans live a healthy and long life thanks to basic foods, including sweet potatoes, soybeans, bitter melon, mugwort, turmeric, and sweet potatoes.

5 **Ogliastra region, Sardinia**: The majority of males who are 100 years old reside in the steep highlands of this Italian island. Its inhabitants follow a low-protein diet linked to decreased incidence of diabetes, cancer, and deaths among those under 65 (*5 "Blue Zones" Where the World's Healthiest People Live*, 2017).

The Blue Zone Way of Life

People who reside in Blue Zones are remarkable for their longevity as well as for how healthy they are. Undoubtedly, they don't achieve this by magic; instead, they engage in several regular habits, nine of which I've mentioned below:

1 **Natural motion**: People who reside in Blue Zone locations exercise often by gardening, walking, and scaling hills and mountains. Many of them continue to live traditionally and avoid utilizing modern technological comforts like washing machines and farming machinery. Exercise is linked to enhanced mental health and quality of life, as well as protection against several chronic diseases like type 2 diabetes, heart disease, and stroke.

2   **Sense of purpose**: Human lifespan and general health and well-being are influenced by one's life purpose, or plan de vida (which translates to "why I wake up in the morning" in Nicoya and Ikigai in Okinawa, respectively). Goal-driven people who live intentionally and reflect on their experiences to further their growth and development are said to have a purpose in life. Having a meaningful purpose in life—whether it is a pastime, rewarding work, or the duty to take care of loved ones—is linked to a host of psychological advantages, such as increased happiness, self-esteem, gratitude, and a positive view of life. According to estimates, having a distinct sense of purpose in life may lengthen your life. Having a purpose in life lowers the risk of all-cause death, according to a study of more than 1,200 elderly citizens living in retirement homes or senior subsidized housing facilities.

3   **Stress reduction**: Although it's practically impossible to completely eliminate stress, persistent stress may have a devastating effect on the body. Chronic stress can exacerbate inflammation and several medical disorders, including heart disease and depression, if it is not treated. The world's longest-living individuals partake in stress-relieving activities like resting, praying, and going to cocktail parties with friends.

4   **80% rule**: The Blue Zone population often eats until their tummies are roughly 80% full to prevent overeating. Many people also skip eating in the evening and spread out their meals throughout the

day. For instance, the Okinawans adhere to the mantra Hara Hachi Bu, which translates to "eat until you're 80% full." Following this straightforward guideline reduces overeating, promotes more conscious eating, and increases lifespan.

5   **Plant-centric diet**: The majority of people who live in Blue Zone locations eat meals that are mostly made of plant-based foods. Usually taken in small amounts, animal proteins are sometimes saved for special occasions. Most of their eating habits are in line with the Mediterranean diet, which emphasizes eating a variety of fruits, vegetables, whole grains, nuts, seeds, beans, and legumes, as well as wholesome oils like extra-virgin olive oil (EVOO). Numerous studies have shown that eating a diet high in plants, like the Mediterranean diet, lowers the risk of death from all causes and the prevalence of depression and cognitive impairment.

6   **Wine consumption**: With the notable exception of the Loma Linda Seventh-Day Adventists in California, many individuals living in the Blue Zones drink modest amounts of wine (one to two glasses each day) with relatives and close friends. Consuming wine as part of a Mediterranean diet has been linked to better disease prognoses and a decreased risk of several chronic health issues, such as type 2 diabetes, age-related cognitive decline, and certain malignancies.

7   **Social networks**: People in their centennial years frequently opt to be members of social groups that promote healthy habits and lifestyles. Sustaining social

connections is crucial for maintaining one's mental and physical health as one age. According to research, socially connected older people have a tendency to maintain their independence, feel more fulfilled in life, and may have less rapid cognitive deterioration than their socially isolated counterparts.

8 **Spirituality**: There are many religious connections among the inhabitants of Blue Zones, but most residents are members of a faith-based group. Weekly religious sessions can lengthen life expectancy by four to fourteen years. According to research, participating in religious services even once a month can have positive effects on one's health. Attending religious services can increase immune system performance and lower your risk of heart disease, among other health advantages. Whatever your religion, spirituality is thought to enhance overall well-being.

9 **Family comes first**: People in Blue Zone regions place high importance on their family bonds. People have dedicated life partners, and parents devote time to their kids. Additionally, it's typical for elderly parents and grandparents to reside with their offspring or other family members to help out with childcare and home tasks. (*The Blue Zones: Lifestyle Habits of the World's Longest-Living Populations*, 2022).

Key Takeaway Points

➢ Recognize the value of whole, unprocessed foods, particularly vegetables. Centenarians often do not adopt a vegan or vegetarian diet, but they do eat primarily plants as a consequence of their reliance on their own cultivated or regionally grown food.

➢ Don't eat packaged or processed foods. When examining the blue zone diets, it becomes clear that they are far lower in sugar, pesticides, and artificial components than the conventional American diet (also known as the SAD).

➢ Create a space that will support healthy living. Starting a "diet" is a common remedy for a growing waistline in the United States and many other industrialized countries, yet none of the centenarians in the blue zones have ever done so, and none of them have ever been overweight. Instead, they just adopted a nutritious diet as a way of life that they shared with others around them. Gaining awareness of your body's genuine hunger cues might help you maintain a healthy weight. The bulk of centenarians in Nicoya, Sardinia, and Okinawa never had the chance to develop the habit of overeating or ingesting a lot of processed foods; instead, throughout most of their lives, they ate little amounts of almost completely unprocessed, unpackaged foods. They take care not to overeat because doing so might be wasteful, deplete the food supply for other family members, and result in a drained, lethargic attitude.

> Engage in frequent, pleasant exercise. Centenarians who live active lives in the blue zones have never stepped into a gym and don't detest working out. They practically live an active lifestyle, walking virtually everywhere (up to five to six miles per day on average), using their hands to complete chores rather than machines, and running errands on foot. They usually stay active by engaging in activities they love, like yoga and tai chi, or by participating in games and athletic activities with friends.

> Create a strong support network to lessen stress. Buettner asserts that surrounding yourself with loved ones and close friends who share your beliefs is arguably the most effective way to modify your lifestyle.

> Spend more time outside and with your family. The individuals who reside in the blue zones appear to value their families above everything else. For instance, Seventh-day Adventists spend time focused on family, God, friendship, and nature during their weekly 24-hour Sabbath. Even though sustained stress can have negative effects on one's health, Adventists assert that their daily activities help them to manage stress, build strong social and family bonds, and obtain regular exercise since the whole family engages in outdoor sports, walks, and other activities (Levy, 2017).

Chapter "Good Will"

Helping others without expectation of anything in return has been proven to lead to increased happiness and satisfaction in life.

I would love to give you the chance to experience that same feeling during your reading or listening experience today...

All it takes is a few moments of your time to answer one simple question:

> **Would you make a difference in the life of someone you've never met—without spending any money or seeking recognition for your good will?**

If so, I have a small request for you.

If you've found value in your reading or listening experience today, I humbly ask that you take a brief moment right now to leave an honest review of this book. It won't cost you anything but 30 seconds of your time—just a few seconds to share your thoughts with others.

Your voice can go a long way in helping someone else find the same inspiration and knowledge that you have.

Are you familiar with leaving a review for an Audible, Kindle, or e-reader book? If so, it's simple:

If you're on **Audible**: just hit the three dots in the top right of your device, click rate & review, then leave a few sentences about the book along with your star rating.

If you're reading on **Kindle** or an e-reader, simply scroll to the last page of the book and swipe up—the review should prompt from there.

If you're on a **Paperback** or any other physical format of this book, you can find the book page on Amazon (or wherever you bought this) and leave your review right there.

Chapter 9

Tales of Youth, Vibrance, and Contentment

The Living Legends of Longevity

I felt that it was essential to incorporate quotes from Octogenarians, Nonagenarians, Centenarians, and Supercentenarians in this last chapter. Reading quotations from these people who are living proof of longevity and hearing their wise counsel and interesting life stories, together with the other material that will be supplied, should inspire you, in my opinion. My goal is to get you all to think about the advice these experts have for young people (or those who are youthful at heart) on how to live not only an extended life but one that is enjoyable. According to some experts, investigating "healthy aging" rather than concentrating on specific diseases may help us uncover genetic or environmental cues that extend and improve life span. Research is now identifying variables that increase the likelihood of healthy aging and turning these discoveries into evidence-based therapies. It is not new to research remarkable human lifespans. It actually has a fascinating past. A study of purported centenarians, some of whom were believed to be older than 160 years, conducted in the early 1970s in the Hunza Valley in Pakistan, the town of Vilcabamba in Ecuador, and the Caucasus area of the former Soviet Union was among the first systematic research on long-lived people. These people were eventually shown to be significantly younger than their reported ages— the majority were, at most, nonagenarians—which raised doubt on the validity of studies on remarkable human lifespans. While these studies did identify a few old individuals who were in good health (and undoubtedly increased yogurt sales), widespread age exaggeration rendered any research on healthy aging in these populations of dubious validity. Furthermore, even if accurate ages could have been obtained, such research would have been difficult due to the primitive condition of aging-related trait quantification, which includes measurement of morbidity, physiological or mental capacity, and impairment. Numerous modifications have been made. We have witnessed a resurgence of interest in the subject of good aging and longevity during the last forty years. The terms "compression of morbidity," "active life expectancy," "effective aging," and "successful aging" are examples of new ideologies. Gerontologists have started measuring longevity using approaches that take into consideration changes in morbidity (diseases), bodily and cognitive abilities, and impairment that occurs with age and throughout time. Initially, these notions were mostly descriptive. At the exact same time, genotyping techniques have advanced from modest studies of potential genes to extensive, intricate whole-genome analysis, gene expression, and much more. As a result, researchers have found what are known as "longevity genes" in both humans and model organisms. Unprecedented developments in proteomes, metabolomes, and several other "omes" are taking place (Willox, 2008).

Quick Tips From Centenarians

Numerous centenarians claim that they feel 20 years younger on average than their actual age and that they do not feel old. Some claim that the key is to act younger than you are! Here are some wise tips from Centenarians:

- ❖ **Maintain an optimistic outlook**: The majority of the centenarians the authors met with identified themselves as upbeat and agreed that maintaining a positive attitude while remaining realistic is important throughout one's life. I believe that having a goal and a passion are equally crucial. The conviction that you can make a difference and the willingness to share your skills with others.

- ❖ **Diet**: Many centenarians advocate eating in moderation rather than promoting a particular diet. No "super-sized meals" from fast-food chains. Others reduced their meat intake or adopted a vegetarian diet.

- ❖ **Exercise**: In terms of lifespan, the adage "move it or lose it" definitely holds true. Find something you want to do... Think about taking up golf or pickleball, going for a stroll, or swimming. It's important to stay moving.

- ❖ **Faith**: The majority of centenarians think that their faith has kept them alive. The majority think they will remain on earth as long as "God" has a plan for them.

❖ **Healthy living**: Nearly 75% of the centenarians surveyed claimed never to have smoked, while the majority of the others quit between the ages of 40 and 70. And while some indicated they never drank, the majority claimed they just occasionally sipped on wine or a drink.

❖ **A devoted family**: Family is the most essential thing for centenarians. They take pride in their responsibilities as patriarchs or matriarchs, and many expressed how rewarding it is to see their younger generations succeed. It's crucial to pass along life lessons, tales, and knowledge to younger family members.

❖ **Genetics**: However, not to be deterred, many centenarians said that their parents and grandparents did not live long lives. It may be a result of choosing the appropriate parents and their DNA. Living "well" may have a bigger impact than we think! (Stewart, 2021).

Additional Statistics You Will Find Interesting

❖ In Japan, there were about 10,000 men and 80,000 women who were 100 years of age or older as of September 2022. In that year, there were around 90.5 thousand centenarians in the nation (*Number of people aged 100 years and older in Japan from 2003 to 2022, by gender*, 2023).

❖ 376 (77%) women and 113 (23%) males make up the 489 Greek centenarians demographics. 1/113 males and 3 percent (11/376) of women were super-centenarians, or older than 110 years (Stathakos, 2005).

❖ One of the five places on earth with the highest concentrations of people who have reached the century mark is Sardinia. On the island, 534 people, or 33.6 per 100,000 residents, are 100 years of age or older (I *'ve lived through hunger and war'*, 2022).

❖ There are currently 626 centenarians living in Costa Rica (Arias, 2017).

❖ In the UK, there were reportedly 15,120 centenarians (those 100 years of age and older) in 2020, up 18% from 2019. The rise in 100-year-olds is what is behind this significant surge in centenarians. Approximately 50% of the population of centenarians in 2020 were 100 years of age or older, compared to an average of 39% during the preceding five years (*Estimates of the very old*, 2021).

Years of Wisdom

Quotes that put a positive spin on aging, which is a perfectly natural process, are nonetheless invaluable in a society where the word "aging" is frequently used in a negative manner. Here are a few memorable quotes (Painter, 2020):

❖ *"Time is only significant if you make it that way."*

❖ *"You don't have to set your alarm clock anymore as you get older."*

❖ *"Celebrate aging since not everyone lives to be this old."*

❖ *"When you take the alternative into account, you'll stop whining about your age."*

❖ *"Only the fortunate get to experience old age."*

❖ *"Wisdom doesn't always accompany advanced age."*

❖ *"Aged and robust like a fine wine sounds better than old age."*

❖ *"Not everyone is aware that although your body may appear older as you age, your soul is still that vivacious, youthful twenty-something."*

❖ *"Old age may sound exhausting and worn out, yet nothing could be farther from reality."*

❖ *"Old age might be the happiest moment of your life since the restrictions of youth are gone."*

❖ *"The experience of becoming older may be quite freeing."*

❖ *"You are vintage, not old."*

❖ *"You don't have to worry about young things when you're old."*

❖ *"Getting older doesn't mean you stop having dreams for the future."*

❖ *"You should still be making plans for the future as you get older."*

❖ *"Don't let anyone tell you that getting older requires you to slow down."*

❖ *"You just have to recognize the power that comes with getting older."*

❖ *"When you get older, you can give wise counsel."*

❖ *"Be proud of your advanced age; many individuals will never be able to."*

❖ *"Be sure to correct someone if they say you're x number of years young; your achievement of living so long should be recognized."*

❖ *"Someone in their twenties coined the expression, 'You're as old as you feel.'"*

❖ *"Celebrate your actual age and be proud of how far you've come."*

❖ *"Stand up! Don't allow becoming older to get you down."*

❖ *"Getting older teaches you to live in the present."*

❖ *"Life is full of wonderful surprises, especially as you get older."*

CONCLUSION

The majority of us aspire to live long lives, but some of you have the caveat that your life should also be full of wellness. It is common for personal ambitions to clash with society's best interests. In this instance, the two are compatible. The overall well-being of humanity is greatly enhanced by longer lifespans, particularly those with healthier and extended lifespans. Your psychological existence is greater as a result of having lived sufficiently long to become acquainted with not just today's generation but a few of those following it, as well as your grandchildren's grandparents. The knowledge and experience of the elderly are beneficial to society. When the young survive to be elderly, the patterns of life are more predictable. Many people discover as they get older that each stage has its own benefits and joys that are rarely imagined when they are younger. Furthermore, it is a type of freedom to live out one's years in good or sufficient health. It provides the chance to ponder, read, work, fall in love, and have fun (Riley, 2015).

By writing this book, I wish to clarify what it means to access your infinity zones, demonstrate that aging is a great and amazing process, and illustrate that it is a true gift. I also hope to show that longevity is not improbable. I don't want you to have any preconceived notions about getting older that are unfavorable; you can still be engaged and active as you age, and you can still enjoy beaches and respect nature. We are all exquisitely and magnificently crafted; cultivate and feed your intellect, care for your physical needs so that you age gracefully and healthily, become involved in your community, feel a part of something, and discover your genuine sense of purpose. With that stated, I'll provide reminders that I want to stick with you, and perhaps you can write them down and post them about your house as affirmations.

The Most Important Things to Remember Regarding Longevity

As I've mentioned, there is a hereditary component to longevity, but environmental influences play a significant role as well. You may enhance the quality and quantity of your life over time by emphasizing things like food and exercise. I want to leave you with a few reminders that you should all keep in mind:

1. **Managing stress**: Because life is unpredictable, we will inevitably face difficult circumstances. You never know when a stressful scenario will arise. The majority of you are aware that stress can negatively affect your health. However, chronic stress could decrease your longevity. I do not want any of you to experience this. I should point out that women who experience high levels of stress have a double risk of developing heart disease, stroke, or lung cancer. As a result, males who are under stress have a threefold increased risk of passing away before their time. Finding a healthy

outlet for your stress is essential because you need to let it out. Yoga, meditation, and tai chi are excellent methods for calming the mind and reducing stress. You can select interests and engage in them regularly if they bring you joy. Writing, drawing, and cooking are all excellent methods to use our energies in a constructive direction.

2   **Nutrition**: One of the best ways to extend your life is to eat healthily. But what does a healthy diet entail? Despite the wide range of dietary choices available, plant-based diets have several amazing advantages that may help people live longer. Higher consumption of plant proteins was linked to a decrease in overall mortality. Replacing animal protein (red or processed meats) with plant protein was linked to decreased chances of overall cancer- and heart disease-related deaths. Increase your intake of vegetables regularly for the aforementioned reasons. Try to include more salads in your meals and more frequently choose plant-based foods in place of meat.

3   **Social connections**: Another essential element of excellent health and well-being is having strong social connections. Our ability to connect with those around us has a significant influence on how joyful we feel every day. A person's lifetime can be extended by having healthy relationships, but it might be decreased by having unhealthy or no social ties. Unexpectedly, the probability of dying increases by 50% for those who don't have close relationships. That is worse than other death risk factors like obesity or inactivity and

comparable to the harmful consequences of smoking. Keep your friends and family nearby and foster wholesome relationships with individuals in your immediate vicinity if you want to benefit from social bonds. Conversely, make an effort to cut back on unhealthy interactions that harm your mental health.

4 **Staying active**: Your likelihood of living a long and healthy life can be greatly increased by maintaining an active lifestyle. This does not, however, imply that you must exercise vigorously each day. Some of the world's longest-living individuals keep busy by performing little tasks around their homes all day. We may keep our blood flowing while we go about our everyday responsibilities by simply going for regular walks, gardening, and completing domestic chores. Make sure to stand up every 20 to 30 minutes if you spend most of the day sitting down. Get some water, take a little rest, or try stretching. It is more probable that you will continue to be active over time if you engage in sports or other activities that you like. You'll be well on your way to developing an active lifestyle if you try to pinpoint some of the things that bring you joy.

5 **Oral health**: You might be surprised to learn how crucial oral health is to our long-term health. Regular oral hygiene practices like brushing and flossing are crucial since there are over 600 different types of germs that may be found in our mouths at any given moment. Left unattended, oral bacteria can cause gum disease, which can make it more likely for your gums to begin bleeding. I know none of you want that.

Through the tightly packed blood vessels in our gums, this bacteria can subsequently spread throughout the remainder of our body, leading to the emergence of several other health issues. Therefore, you must take excellent care of your mouth if you want to live long, healthy lives. You may have a positive effect on the world by taking care of your dental health. Taking care of our dental health has several benefits, including:

- ❖ Inflammation and toxin levels in our bodies
- ❖ Our circulatory system and heart are burdened by inflammation.
- ❖ How steadfast we are against dementia
- ❖ Maternity health

A quick dental tip: To prevent oral health problems from developing, try to floss every day, clean your teeth, and visit the dentist frequently (Maneeza, 2023):

1 **Eat like an Okinawan**: The inhabitants of Okinawa, Japan, have the longest life spans on the planet. The reason for this is the local diet. It has few calories and is rich in green and yellow veggies. Additionally, some Okinawans had the practice of just consuming 80% of the food on their plates. Because they no longer practice the ancient methods, younger generations aren't living as long.

2 **Welcome naps**: Many cultures throughout the world have siestas as a norm, and now there is scientific proof that resting may extend your life. According to one study, those who regularly zzz'd had a 37% lower

risk of passing away from heart disease than others who did so only occasionally. Researchers believe that by reducing stress chemicals, naps may benefit your heart.

3 **Quit smoking**: You already know that quitting smoking may prolong your life, but you might be surprised at how much longer. According to 50-year-old British research, giving up at age 30 may buy you a whole decade. You can live an additional 9, 6, or 3 years if you stop the habit at age 40, 50, or 60, respectively.

4 **Make friends**: Another good reason to be thankful for your friends is the possibility that they will extend your life. Numerous studies demonstrate a direct connection between robust social connections and an extended lifespan. Therefore, set aside time to stay in touch.

5 **Choose your friends wisely**: Look for people who lead healthy lifestyles since your friends' behaviors will influence you. If you have a friend who puts on weight, your chances of developing weight gain increase. Smoking spreads through social networks as well but giving up is just as infectious.

6 **Pay attention to detail**: According to 80-year research, conscientious individuals live longer because they pay attention to the little things, consider their options, and make an effort to do the right thing. They take better care of themselves, and they choose to

have healthier relationships and more fulfilling employment.

7   **Shed a few pounds**: If you're overweight, losing weight can help you avoid problems like diabetes, heart disease, and others that shorten your lifespan. Focus on flattening that chubby tummy since belly fat is unhealthy for you. To lose belly fat, increase your fiber intake and exercise frequently.

8   **Drink in moderation**: People who drink in moderation are less likely to get heart disease than those who never touch alcohol. On the other side, consuming too much alcohol can result in weight gain, increased blood pressure, and a variety of other health issues. If you don't already drink, please hold off! Alcohol has more negative effects than positive ones. Limit your alcohol consumption if you do.

9   **Get spiritual**: I know it sounds cliché, but people who regularly attend religious services typically live longer than non-religious people. In a 12-year study of adults over 65, those who visited more frequently than once a week had greater levels of a crucial immune system protein than their counterparts who didn't. The strong connection to others that forms among congregants may improve your health.

10   **Practice the art of forgiveness**: Surprisingly, letting go of resentment is good for your physical health. Heart disease, stroke, deteriorating lung function, and other issues are all connected to chronic rage. You'll feel less anxious, have lower blood pressure, and have

easier breathing if you can forgive. With age, the benefits usually increase.

11 **Make sleep your best friend**: You can reduce your chances of obesity, diabetes, heart disease, and mental disorders by getting enough good sleep. Additionally, it will hasten your recovery from disease. On the other side, working through the night is unhealthy. Make sleep a priority because getting less than five hours a night might increase your risk of dying young.

12 **Maintain a sense of purpose**: Your life may last longer if you enjoy meaningful hobbies and pursuits. A person with a strong sense of purpose has a lower risk of dying from heart disease or a stroke than someone with a weaker sense of self. Having a good understanding of your actions and their motivations might help reduce your risk of developing Alzheimer's disease (Felson, 2022).

Longevity Increases by Practicing Meditation

Imagine living longer and appreciating your life—your family, friends, food, and the outdoors—without having to pursue everlasting life and the fountain of youth, which are ancient myths. If you don't want to live forever, why not try to live longer and happier by taking positive action? Happy news: you can. According to several studies conducted over many years, mindfulness meditation can increase life expectancy. Meditation has been scientifically shown to reduce stress, which significantly lowers the likelihood of encountering certain triggers. According to research conducted in 1989, meditation helps older folks live longer, be healthier, and have better brains. The average age of the 70 elderly individuals was 81. For three years, they either meditated twice daily for 20 minutes, performed relaxation or mental activities, or did nothing. Meditation practitioners experienced lower blood pressure and better mental wellness. No members of the meditation group passed away over the three years of the study. The elderly who meditated also reported feeling younger, having greater problem-solving skills, and having more patience. A hectic schedule causes weight gain and stress. When living in the now feels difficult or forgotten, we are frequently pressed for time because of our habits. You may increase your lifespan, lead a more satisfying existence, and feel alive by adding the practice of mindfulness meditation to your life. Instead of spending money on expensive drugs and concoctions that promise to extend your life, just permit yourself to be conscious. Why not give it a try? (Dyson, 2023)

Foods to Eat That Can Contribute to Your Longevity

Below are reminders of some foods to eat to keep you and your loved ones healthy, happy, and active. I urge you all to make informed food decisions since what we eat affects how long we live:

1 **Berries**: These are a fantastic source of antioxidants and may help fend against various brain illnesses as well as cancer. They also exist in frozen berries. You can find them in the freezer section of the grocery store and eat them all year.

2 **Extra virgin olive oil**: This delicious "good" fat may have antioxidant and anti-inflammatory qualities.

According to certain research, it could lower cholesterol levels.

3 **Fish**: It has been dubbed "brain food" because the fatty acids DHA and EPA in it can support healthy neurological and cognitive function. You could be less likely to develop dementia if you eat fish one or two times a week. Salmon and trout are examples of fatty fish that contain omega-3 fats that help reduce "bad" cholesterol and triglycerides. Additionally, it might lessen the inflammation brought on by fatty deposits clogging your arteries, which causes atherosclerosis.

4 **Beans**: Include these food groups at least three to four times each week in your diet. The fiber may aid in digestion and reduce your risk of diabetes, heart disease, and obesity. A diet rich in fiber may also aid in weight loss since it helps you feel fuller for longer. Use chickpeas as a salad topping or substitute beans for meat in soups.

5 **Vegetables**: Vegetables include tons of vitamins and minerals, fiber, and antioxidants that may help shield you from chronic illnesses. Strong bones are aided by the vitamin K in dark, leafy greens. Vitamin A, found in both sweet potatoes and carrots, aids in the maintenance of healthy skin, eyes, and immune systems.

6 **Nuts**: Nuts are a rich source of other nutrients and cholesterol-free plant protein. Pecans contain antioxidants, while almonds are high in vitamin E, which can help lessen women's risk of stroke. Walnuts'

unsaturated fats can help boost HDL cholesterol and reduce LDL cholesterol. However, nuts include some fat. There are 160 calories in one ounce of almonds or around 24 nuts. So, indulge in them sparingly.

7   **Dairy**: Milk and other beverages with vitamin D fortification assist your body in absorbing and using calcium. This is crucial if you have osteoporosis, which causes the bones to thin. To aid with digestion, consume yogurt with living cultures.

8   **Whole grains**: Your risk of developing some cancers, type 2 diabetes, and heart disease may be reduced by including these in your diet. Additionally, fiber may lessen the likelihood of digestive issues, including diverticulitis and constipation. Select whole-grain pastas and breads, and brown or wild rice in place of white rice. Add plain oats to meatloaf or soups if you want to include barley.

9   **Maintain a healthy weight**: As they age, some people find it challenging to maintain their weight, particularly after an illness or accident. Smaller meals spaced out by wholesome snacks are two suggestions, as is moving to whole milk from skim. Avoid eating a lot of meals that are heavy in fat or sugar since you won't obtain the nutrients you need if you do (Khatri, 2020).

Don't Forget to Embrace Positive Thinking

Staying optimistic takes practice, just like meditation, yoga, or any other self-care regimen. Fortunately, the necessary tools are free, and you may use them independently at your own speed. Here are a few strategies for actively cultivating optimistic thinking in your day-to-day life (Stibich, 2020):

1 **Keep a gratitude diary**: A gratitude journal may be an effective approach to connecting with your emotions and reducing stress, regardless of the style you choose—brief notes on your phone or lengthy entries written in a notebook. The key is consistency, regardless of the topic. Regular practice will assist in forming a new style of thinking that will make it simple for you to spot and dismiss unfavorable thoughts as they enter your head.

2 **Repeat positive affirmations**: You are more inclined to believe anything if you repeat it often enough. Positive affirmations, which include phrases like "I am feeling calmer each day" and "I am capable of handling whatever comes my way," are meant to do just that. They are statements that are repeated repeatedly with the purpose of changing. Keep these affirmations grounded in reality at all times. Your subconscious mind could raise a red flag for implausible claims, sending you back into a bad mood.

3 **Practice loving-kindness meditation**: According to studies, practicing loving-kindness meditation may considerably boost one's disposition. Although there are several variants to the practice, the main idea is to

concentrate on words and phrases that encourage empathy for oneself as well as for others, such as "*may I be joyful*" and "*may you be protected.*"

4 **Spend time with others who share a positive outlook on life**: It's been said that "you are influenced by the company you keep." Therefore, it makes sense that being around other optimists helps you feel inspired, joyful, and encouraged. Observe your feelings while you are around friends and relatives. You might need to set restrictions with those who make you feel negative energy.

5 **Remember that being positive is a choice—and not necessarily a simple one**: It may be challenging to keep a positive outlook on life at times, and you can experience days when you lack any optimism. But with time and effort, you may lay a foundation that makes it easier for you to change your perspective and begin observing changes in your psychological, emotional, and physical well-being.

The most costly resource currently is time. We are all given a finite amount of time in this life, and we cannot turn back the hands of time. We can only focus on the present moment and what lies ahead now that everything has been completed. We want our bodies, minds, and souls to be at their best since we only have a limited amount of time to accomplish the objectives and goals we want to attain as well as live this life to the fullest. Although our starting point is genetics, our surroundings and way of life have a significant impact on how long we live. Our vitality will increase with improved living conditions and healthy lives. We all understand the benefits of living a healthy lifestyle but putting it into practice in our day-to-day activities may be difficult. We all know we need to exercise for at least 30 minutes every day, but it can be difficult to find the time, energy, and drive to do so. But I'm confident you can figure it out once you all shift your perspectives and challenge yourselves. We are aware that we should consume lean meat, more water, less alcohol, and greater quantities of vegetables and fruits, yet at the end of a long, exhausting day at work, we seek the simplest, fastest processed fast-food that is readily available (Powell, 2020).

I know what you're going through; I really do, but I want you to get out of your comfort zone and start planning and making meals because you can do so much more. I know you all want to live longer and in better health, but creating a healthy environment and developing healthy living habits are not as simple. However, if you tap into your infinity zones and put the numerous things I've listed into practice, you will succeed. It's time to take a closer look and begin weighing your present health and life against where you genuinely want your vitality to be. Make the most of your life because you only have one to live! Make a commitment to modifying your way of life in small, lasting ways so that you might live a long, fulfilling life. I hope my book has given you the information and motivation you need to have a full, happy, and healthy life.

Share your thoughts by leaving a review. Your feedback will help others discover the benefits of unlocking infinity and mastering the art of longevity.

Chapter "Good Will"

Helping others without expectation of anything in return has been proven to lead to increased happiness and satisfaction in life.

I would love to give you the chance to experience that same feeling during your reading or listening experience today...

All it takes is a few moments of your time to answer one simple question:

> Would you make a difference in the life of someone you've never met—without spending any money or seeking recognition for your good will?

If so, I have a small request for you.

If you've found value in your reading or listening experience today, I humbly ask that you take a brief moment right now to leave an honest review of this book. It won't cost you anything but 30 seconds of your time—just a few seconds to share your thoughts with others.

Your voice can go a long way in helping someone else find the same inspiration and knowledge that you have.

Are you familiar with leaving a review for an Audible, Kindle, or e-reader book? If so, it's simple:

If you're on **Audible**: just hit the three dots in the top right of your device, click rate & review, then leave a few sentences about the book along with your star rating.

If you're reading on **Kindle** or an e-reader, simply scroll to the last page of the book and swipe up—the review should prompt from there.

If you're on a **Paperback** or any other physical format of this book, you can find the book page on Amazon (or wherever you bought this) and leave your review right there.

SPREAD THE WORD!

You're about to begin a life-changing journey… and that puts you in the perfect position to help someone else along on theirs.

Simply by sharing your honest opinion of this book and a little about your own journey, you'll show new readers where they can find the keys to a long and healthy life.

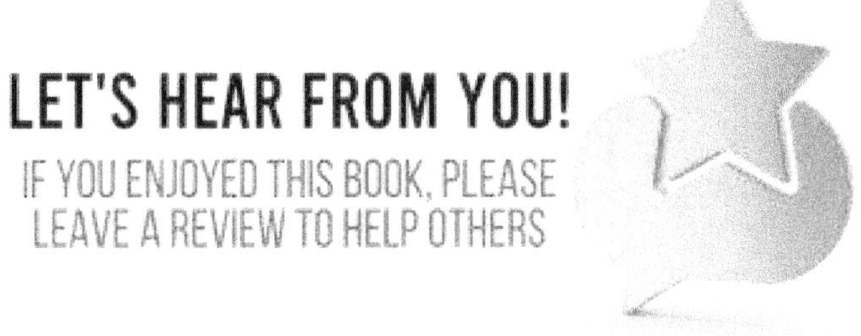

Thank you for your support. I wish you all the best going forward.

REFERENCES

Abedi, R. (2023, April 27). *Difference between chronological and biological age: reverse your aging.* Health Longevity Clinic (HLC). https://www.healthylongevity.clinic/blog/chronological-vs-biological-age-difference

Ackerman, C.E. (2017, January 18). *21 mindfulness exercises & activities for adults.* Positive Psychology. https://positivepsychology.com/mindfulness-exercises-techniques-activities/

Ackerman, C.E. (2020, April 1). *What is self-awareness? (+5 ways to be more self-aware).* Positive Psychology. https://positivepsychology.com/self-awareness-matters-how-you-can-be-more-self-aware/

Akinola, S. (2021, March 30). *What is the biggest benefit technology will have on ageing and longevity?* World Economic Forum. https://www.weforum.org/agenda/2021/03/what-is-the-biggest-benefit-technology-ageing-longevity-global-future-council-tech-for-good/

Arias, L. (2017, July 13). *Costa Rica studies longevity of its centenarian citizens.* Tico Times.

https://ticotimes.net/2017/07/13/longevity-centenarian-costa-rica#:~:text=Data%20from%20the%20National%20Institute,centenarians%20living%20in%20Costa%20Rica.

Basaraba, S. (2023, February 13). *Chronological vs. biological age: understanding the differences and factors that affect your health.* Very Well Health. https://www.verywellhealth.com/what-is-chronological-age-2223384

Bueno, M. (2023, May). *How to unfold your infinite potential: a guide to unlocking your true self.* Medium. https://medium.com/@miriam.buenoo/how-to-unfold-your-infinite-potential-a-guide-to-unlocking-your-true-self-61663d3eca35

Buettner, D., Skemp, S. (2019, July). Blue zones: lessons from the world's longest lived. *National Library of Medicine, 10*, p. 318-321

Can you lengthen your life? (June 2016). News in Health. https://newsinhealth.nih.gov/2016/06/can-you-lengthen-your-life

Caturla, N. PhD. (2021, October 1). *The ins and outs of aging: intrinsic/extrinsic factors and nutricosmetic fixes.* Cosmetics and Toiletries. https://www.cosmeticsandtoiletries.com/research/literature-data/article/21836451/the-ins-and-outs-of-aging-intrinsicextrinsic-factors-and-nutricosmetic-fixes

Crimmins, E.M. (2015, December). Lifespan and health span: past, present, and promise. *National Library of Medicine, 55*, 901-9011. https://www.ncbi.nlm.nih.gov/pmc/articles/PMC4 861644/

Dazu, V. (2021, March 30). *The chance to age in place.* World Economic Forum. https://www.weforum.org/agenda/2021/03/what-is-the-biggest-benefit-technology-ageing-longevity-global-future-council-tech-for-good/

Dolgoff, S. (2021, March 6). *Stop believing these longevity myths to live a longer, healthier, and happier life.* Prevention. https://www.prevention.com/health/a35217718/lo ngevity-myths/

Doron, T. (2020, April 8). *Science of social connection.* RO. https://ro.co/health-guide/friends-and-longevity/

Dyson, T. (2023, July 30). *Meditation lengthens life expectancy.* Tracy Quantum Consulting. https://www.tracyquantum.com/blog/benefits-of-meditation/life-expectancy

Ellerbeck, S. (2023, February 22). *5 innovations that are revolutionizing global healthcare.* World Economic Forum. https://www.weforum.org/agenda/2023/02/health -future-innovation-technology/

Estimates of the very old, including centenarians, UK: 2002 to 2020. (2021, September 23). Office for National Statistics. https://www.ons.gov.uk/peoplepopulationandcom munity/birthsdeathsandmarriages/ageing/bulletins/

estimatesoftheveryoldincludingcentenarians/2002to
2020#:~:text=There%20were%20an%20estimated
%2015%2C120,in%20100%2Dyear%2Dolds.

5 "blue zones" where the world's healthiest people live. (2017, April
6). National Geographic.
https://www.nationalgeographic.com/books/article
/5-blue-zones-where-the-worlds-healthiest-people-
live

Felson, S. (2022, November 27). *18 secrets for a longer life.*
WebMD. https://www.webmd.com/healthy-
aging/ss/slideshow-longer-life-secrets

Garland, R. (2020, November 27). *Life expectancy of the Ancient
Greeks.* Wondrium Daily.
https://www.wondriumdaily.com/life-expectancy-
of-the-ancient-greeks/

Hall, W., Lucke, J.C. (2005, February). Who wants to live
forever? *National Library of Medicine, 6*, 98-102.
https://www.ncbi.nlm.nih.gov/pmc/articles/PMC1
299249/

Hashmi, M. (2021, March 30). *Multichannel health delivery...built
around the individual.* World Economic Forum.
https://www.weforum.org/agenda/2021/03/what-
is-the-biggest-benefit-technology-ageing-longevity-
global-future-council-tech-for-good/

*Healthy heart, healthy mind: understanding the connection between
mental health and your body.* (2023). Jefferson Center.
https://www.jcmh.org/healthy-heart-healthy-mind-
understanding-the-connection-between-mental-
health-and-your-body/

Hetherington, C. PhD. (2023, June 2). *The power of social connection for longevity*. Healthnews. https://healthnews.com/longevity/healthspan/social-connection-and-longevity/

Hicks, P. (2021, March 30). *Allowing older persons to fully exercise their human rights*. World Economic Forum. https://www.weforum.org/agenda/2021/03/what-is-the-biggest-benefit-technology-ageing-longevity-global-future-council-tech-for-good/

How technology will impact aging now and the near future. (2023). Leonard Davis, School of Gerontology. https://gero.usc.edu/students/current-students/careers-in-aging/how-technology-will-impact-aging-now-and-the-near-future/

I've lived through hunger and war': tiny Italian town sets record as 10th resident turns 100. (2022, February 14). The Guardian. https://www.theguardian.com/world/2022/feb/14/10-residents-over-100-record-breaking-sardinia-town-perdasdefogu#:~:text=Sardinia%20has%20been%20identified%20as,33.6%20for%20every%20100%2C000%20inhabitants.

Infinity symbol meaning in modern times. (2019, April 4). Gyllen. https://gyllenwatches.com/blogs/journal/infinity-symbol-meaning#:~:text=Infinity%20Symbol%20Meaning%20in%20Spirituality%20and%20Meditation,-Infinity%20holds%20a&text=Life%20is%20infinite.,harmony%2C%20peace%2C%20and%20oneness.

Johnson, J. (2019, August 15). *How to improve your memory: 8 techniques to try.* Medical News Today. https://www.medicalnewstoday.com/articles/326068

Johnson, J. (2023, April 4). *22 brain exercises to improve memory, cognition, and creativity.* Medical News Today. https://www.medicalnewstoday.com/articles/brain-exercises

Kero, A. (2023, March 27). *10 things you can do to nourish your soul.* Everyday Power. https://everydaypower.com/things-to-nourish-your-soul-2-2/

Khatri, M. (2020, December 17). *Foods for a long, healthy life.* WebMD. https://www.webmd.com/healthy-aging/ss/slideshow-nutrition-longevity

Kirkwood, B.L. (2005, February 25). *Understanding the odd science of aging.* Cell. https://www.cell.com/fulltext/S0092-8674(05)00101-7

Levy, J. (2017, June 21). *Blue zones secrets — how to live 100+ years.* Dr. Axe. https://draxe.com/health/blue-zones/

Longo, V. (2018, January). *What exercise is best for optimal health and longevity?* Blue Zones. https://www.bluezones.com/2018/01/what-exercise-best-happy-healthy-life/

Maneeza, H. (2023). *The keys to longevity: 5 ways to age well through life.* Montes Medical Group.

https://www.montesmedical.com/the-keys-to-longevity-5-ways-to-age-well-through-life/

Merchant, J. (2016, December 29). *Encyclopedia of personality and individual differences.* Springer Link. https://link.springer.com/referenceworkentry/10.1007/978-3-319-28099-8_1361-1

Morgan, L.A., Kunkel, S.R. (2015). *Aging, society, and the life course, fifth edition.* Springer Publishing Company.

Nania, R. (2020, October 27). *5 Myths about brain health and aging.* AARP. https://www.aarp.org/health/brain-health/info-2020/brain-health-myths.html

Number of people aged 100 years and older in Japan from 2003 to 2022, by gender. (2023, February 28). Statista. https://www.statista.com/statistics/1172781/japan-number-centenarians-by-gender/#:~:text=Number%20of%20people%20aged%20100,Japan%202003%2D2022%2C%20by%20gender&text=As%20of%20September%202022%2C%20around,90.5%20thousand%20in%20the%20country.

O'Connor, A. (2022, October 18). *At any age, a healthy diet can extend your life.* The Washington Post. https://www.washingtonpost.com/wellness/2022/10/18/healthy-eating-aging/

Oppland, M. (2017, April 28). *13 most popular gratitude exercises & activities.* Positive Psychology. https://positivepsychology.com/gratitude-exercises/

Painter, S. (2020, October 1). *60+ inspirational old age quotes.* Love to Know. https://www.lovetoknow.com/quotes-quips/relationships/good-senior-quotes

Pal, S., Tyler, J.K. (2016, July 19). *Epigenetics and aging.* Science Advances. https://www.science.org/doi/10.1126/sciadv.16005 84#:~:text=Among%20these%20hallmarks%2C%2 0epigenetic%20alterations,of%20the%20underlying %20DNA%20sequence.

Petre, A. (2023, March 16). *Habits to form now for a longer life.* Healthline. https://www.healthline.com/nutrition/13-habits-linked-to-a-long-life

Pietrangelo, A., Raypole, C. (2023, February 16). *What are the effects of alcohol on the body?* Healthline. https://www.healthline.com/health/alcohol/effects -on-body

Positive thinking: stop negative self-talk to reduce stress. (2022, February 3). Mayo Clinic. https://www.mayoclinic.org/healthy-lifestyle/stress-management/in-depth/positive-thinking/art-20043950

Powell, A. (2022, April 20). *Thoughts on longevity.* LinkedIn. https://www.linkedin.com/pulse/thoughts-longevity-amanda-powell/

Psychological age. (2023, March 20). CEOpedia Management. https://ceopedia.org/index.php/Psychological_age

Rai, A. (2023, July 30). *One soul, one infinity: the boundless nature of consciousness*. Medium. https://medium.com/@avinash31d/one-soul-one-infinity-the-boundless-nature-of-consciousness-6b8a5fd7ae1e

Riley, J.C. (2015, February 5). *Rising life expectancy*. Cambridge Core. https://www.cambridge.org/core/books/abs/rising-life-expectancy/conclusion/903275211AF71CEF440D8714090CA20D

Robertson, R. PhD. (2017, August 29). *Why people in "blue zones" live longer than the rest of the world*. Healthline. https://www.healthline.com/nutrition/blue-zones

Robertson, R. PhD. (2023, January 23). *9 ways to improve your gut bacteria, based on science*. Healthline. https://www.healthline.com/nutrition/improve-gut-bacteria

Roiss, S. (2020, November 23). *Spiritual meaning of the infinity symbol*. Medium. https://medium.com/@office.sparklshop/spiritual-meaning-of-the-infinity-symbol-fa69465c6110#:~:text=The%20symbol%20of%20infinity%20has,have%20in%20front%20of%20us.

Scott, A.J. (2021, December). The Longevity Society. *Pub Med, 12*, 820-827. https://pubmed.ncbi.nlm.nih.gov/36098038/

Shrestha, R. (2022, August 8). *Ageing: types, stages, causes, signs, health problems and solutions.* Public Health Notes. https://www.publichealthnotes.com/ageing/

Social interaction and longevity amongst seniors. (2022, January 31). Welbe Health. https://welbehealth.com/social-interaction/

Societal aging. (2022, October 31). World Bank. https://www.worldbank.org/en/topic/pensions/brief/societal-aging

Stathakos, D., Pratsinis, H., Zachos, I., Irene Vlahaki, I., Gianakopoulou, A., Dimitra Z., Dimitris, K. (2005, June). Greek centenarians: Assessment of functional health status and life-style characteristics. *Science Direct, 40,* 512-518. https://www.sciencedirect.com/science/article/abs/pii/S0531556505000586#:~:text=The%20demographic%20characteristics%20of%20the,aged%20110%20years%20or%20more.

Steven. (2013, December 12). *The infinity symbol: a timeless emblem of limitlessness.* Cuded. https://www.cuded.com/infinity-symbol/

Stewart, S. (2021, April 30). *Words of wisdom from centenarians.* Tuscon. Com. https://tucson.com/article_33aae1d4-98c2-11eb-b516-83c7ce4e4265.html

Stibich, M. (2020, February 4). *Embrace aging with positive thinking.* Very Well Mind. https://www.verywellmind.com/positive-thinking-and-aging-2224134

Stibich, M. PhD. (2023, April, 5). *How you can increase your longevity*. Very Well Health.
https://www.verywellhealth.com/what-is-longevity-2223930#:~:text=Longevity%20is%20defined%20as%20%22long,who%20lives%20a%20long%20time.

Symons, D.K. (2011). *Psychological Age*. Encyclopedia of Child Behavior and Development. Springer, Boston, MA
https://link.springer.com/referenceworkentry/10.1007/978-0-387-79061-9_2298#:~:text=Description,older%20than%20they%20really%20are.

The 7 biggest longevity myths. (2023, March 22). Novos.
https://novoslabs.com/the-7-biggest-longevity-myths/

The blue zones: lifestyle habits of the world's longest-living populations. (2022, September 15). Fullscript.
https://fullscript.com/blog/blue-zones

The elixir of youth': Science explains how humans can live longer. (2021, October 29). World Economic Forum.
https://www.weforum.org/agenda/2021/10/life-extension-health-ageing?DAG=3&gclid=Cj0KCQjw756lBhDMARIsAEI0Agmi28xABwEh-XsidhEyKCIeuzpJDG6GiXJ99aYgBmVLUc6-TufauOQaApvlEALw_wcB

The future of public health. (1988). Institute of Medicine (US) Committee for the Study of the Future of Public Health. National Academic Press. National Library of Medicine.

https://www.ncbi.nlm.nih.gov/books/NBK218218/

The mind-body connection: how mental health impacts longevity and quality of life. (2023, May 17). Novos. https://novoslabs.com/mental-health-impact-on-longevity/#:~:text=Mental%20health%20is%20an%20essential,risk%20of%20age%2Drelated%20diseases.

The ultimate guide to creating a longevity plan for a healthy and fulfilling life. (2023). NAO Medical. https://naomedical.com/info/ultimate-guide-longevity-plan-healthy-life.html

What are blue zones? (2023). Wonderopolis. https://wonderopolis.org/wonder/What-Are-Blue-Zones

What is brain health and why is the brain important? (2023) Your Heights. https://www.yourheights.com/blog/health/what-is-brain-health-and-why-does-it-matter/

Willcox, B.J., Willcox, D.C., Ferrucci, L. (2008, November 1). Secrets of healthy aging and longevity from exceptional survivors around the globe: lessons from octogenarians to supercentenarians. *Oxford Academic, 63,* 1181-1185. https://academic.oup.com/biomedgerontology/article/63/11/1181/759344

Winslow, C. E. A. (1923). *The evolution and significance of the modern public health campaign.* Journal of Public Health Policy, South Burlington, Vt.

Zhang, S., Duan, E. (2018, April 25). *Fighting against skin aging.* *National Library of Medicine, 5,* 729-738. https://www.ncbi.nlm.nih.gov/pmc/articles/PMC6047276/#:~:text=Intrinsic%20aging%20is%20an%20inevitable,wrinkles%2C%20loss%20of%20elasticity%2C%20laxity

ABOUT THE AUTHOR

This author has a knack for capturing the essence of life's complexities, intricacies, and universal truths through her writing, often presenting thought-provoking perspectives on various aspects of existence. Her life books are characterized by rich character development, as the author skillfully weaves together the stories of diverse topics, illuminating journeys, challenges, and triumphs. Through books, the author explores themes such as love, passion, victory, identity, personal growth, and the search for meaning, offering readers profound insights and moments of introspection.

Beyond Zoë's professional accomplishments, she also has a rich and multifaceted life outside of publishing. This book is a testament to her commitment to providing valuable insights and practical guidance. The author's books are often praised for their ability to evoke empathy in readers, fostering a deep connection between the readers and the valuable insights they encounter within the pages.

The author is a distinguished authority in various fields of study, bringing a wealth of knowledge and experience to her thought-provoking non-fiction works. As you delve into Zoë's manuscripts, you can expect to embark on an intellectual journey guided by Zoë's profound insights and intentional thought-provoking passion for self -development. Her non-fiction works continue to push the boundaries of knowledge, inviting readers to expand their horizons and gain a deeper understanding of life and its impact on our success.

Zoë's works have been praised for their meticulous research, insightful analysis, and the way they challenge readers to think critically about the world around them.

Any one of Zoë's latest books….

1. Longevity: The Art of Aging Backwards
Step-by-Step Guide to Renew, Restore and Reverse Aging Mentally, Physically & Spiritually

2. Living Your Best Life: Radiate from Within
Ultimate Guide to Finding Purpose & Fulfillment in 3 Easy Steps.

3. Alone, But Not Lonely: Aging on Your Terms
A Roadmap for Aging Independently, Striking Balance & Finding Purpose

4. Redefining Aging: The Art of Living Alone
How to Find Joy in Independence, Live Fearlessly & Maintain Longevity

5. Journeying Alone, Journeying Strong: Navigating Aging Alone Without Children
Self-Help Guide to Finding Inner Strength, Peace, Joy & Fulfillment in Childless Aging

6. Mastering the Steps to Success: Achieving Success at Every Rung
Proven Strategies for Overcoming Obstacles and Reaching Greatness. Develop, Learn, Succeed

7. The Positivity Code: Supercharge Your Life with Positive Thinking
Learn The Art of Positive Thinking, Changing Your Life One Thought at a Time

8. The Growth Mindset Code: Cracking the Secrets to Success
Comprehensive Guide to Breaking Limits with A Growth Mindset, Cultivating Unlimited Possibilities

9. The Superfood Prescription: Refuel Your Mind & Body
100 Supercharged Foods to Revitalize & Transform Your Health

… is another testament to her dedication to delivering enlightening and captivating non-fiction literature. Whether you're a seasoned reader of non-fiction or new to the genre Zoë's work is sure to engage, inform, and inspire.

To stay updated on **Zoë Publishing's** latest projects and musings, visit us on *www.facebook.com/zoepublishing* and follow us on Instagram & Tik Tok **(@zoepublishing)**

* 9 7 9 8 2 2 4 1 6 3 5 0 2 *